CIVILIZATION:

ETHICS, LAW, SOCIETY, ECONOMICS

**George D. Merrill
Donald J. Haley
Myron L. Kennedy
Robert C. Putzel**

El Camino College
Torrance, California

KENDALL/HUNT PUBLISHING COMPANY
2460 Kerper Boulevard   P.O. Box 539   Dubuque, Iowa 52004-0539

Copyright © 1976 by George D. Merrill, Donald J. Haley, Myron L. Kennedy, and Robert C. Putzel

Library of Congress Catalog Card Number: 76-20920

ISBN 0-8403-2679-3

All rights reserved. No part of this publication may be reproduced, stored in a retrieval system, or transmitted, in any form or by any means, electronic, mechanical, photocopying, recording, or otherwise, without the prior written permission of the copyright owner.

Printed in the United States of America
10 9 8 7 6

CONTENTS

Preface, **vii**

I. **Ancient Civilization, 1**
   A. ETHICS, **1**
   1. Akkadian Creation Epic, **1**
   2. Creation According to Genesis, **4**
   3. Hesiod's Creation Epic, **6**
   4. Stoicism of Marcus Aurelius, **8**

   B. LAW, **10**
   5. Code of Hammurabi, **10**
   6. The Ten Commandments, **11**
   7. Spartan Constitution, Plutarch, **12**
   8. Athenian Democracy, Pericles, **13**
   9. Roman Constitution, Polybius, **14**

   C. SOCIETY, **16**
   10. Egyptian Social Customs, Herodotus, **16**
   11. Hazards of City Life in Rome, Juvenal, **17**
   12. A Roman Banquet, Petronius, **18**

   D. ECONOMICS, **20**
   13. Economic Advantages of Athens, Xenophon, **20**
   14. Economic Decline of Rome, Ferdinand Lot, **21**

   E. SOURCES FOR PART I, **26**

II. **Medieval Civilization, 29**
   A. ETHICS, **29**
   1. Sermon on the Mount, **29**
   2. Revelations of Mohammed, **32**
   3. Medieval Mysticism, St. Francis of Assissi, **33**
   4. On the Existence of God, St. Thomas Aquinas, **34**

   B. LAW, **36**
   5. Salic Law, **36**
   6. Justinian's Institutes, **37**

       7. Administrative Directives of Charlemagne, **38**
       8. Feudal Contracts, **40**
       9. Peace and Truce of God, **41**
     10. Magna Carta, **42**
  C. SOCIETY, **44**
     11. Description of a Serf, France—13th Century, **44**
     12. Fourteenth Century Plague, Boccaccio, **44**
     13. Ordinance Concerning Laborers and Servants, England—1349, **45**
     14. Serf Family, Creed of Piers Plowman, **46**
  D. ECONOMICS, **47**
     15. The Wealth of Constantinople, Robert of Clari, **47**
     16. Guild Restrictions, **47**
  E. SOURCES FOR PART II, **48**

III. **Renaissance Civilization, 51**
  A. ETHICS, **51**
      1. In Praise of Folly, Erasmus, **51**
      2. Ninety-five Theses, Luther, **53**
      3. Institutes, of the Christian Religion, **54**
      4. Catholic Reformation, Council of Trent, **56**
  B. LAW, **58**
      5. Peasant Demands, **58**
      6. City of God on Earth, Ordinances of Geneva, **59**
      7. A Declaration of Independence, Holland, **60**
  C. SOCIETY, **61**
      8. Advice to a Teenage Cardinal, Lorenzo de Medici, **61**
      9. Corruption Among the Clergy, Savanarola, **61**
     10. The Parisians, Rabelais, **62**
     11. Pride of the Artisan, Cellini, **63**
     12. Acceptance of Black Magic, Cellini, **63**
     13. Nobility at Home, Castiglione, **64**
  D. ECONOMICS, **64**
     14. Revenues of Renaissance Rulers, **64**
     15. Book of Husbandry (1523), Fitzherbert, **66**
     16. Draft of a Poor Law (1536), William Marshall, **66**
     17. Early Mercantilism, Thomas Mun, **67**
  E. SOURCES FOR PART III, **68**

IV. **Enlightened Civilization, 71**
  A. ETHICS, **71**
      1. Religion and Liberty, Spinoza, **71**
      2. A Philosophical Dictionary, Voltaire, **73**
      3. Reflections of a Deist, Franklin, **76**

    B. LAW, **78**
- 4. Bill of Rights, England—1689, **78**
- 5. Declaration of Rights, France—1789, **79**
- 6. Bill of Rights, United States—1791, **80**

    C. SOCIETY, **81**
- 7. A Young Lady of Fashion's Day—1712, **81**
- 8. Court Life at Versailles, Saint-Simon, **82**
- 9. Napoleon's Wardrobe for 1811-12, **83**

    D. ECONOMICS, **85**
- 10. English Tradesman, Defoe, **85**
- 11. Economic Liberty, Adam Smith, **87**
- 12. English Commerce, Voltaire, **88**
- 13. State of English Agriculture in 1770, **90**

    E. SOURCES FOR PART IV, **90**

V. Modern Civilization, 93

    A. ETHICS, **93**
- 1. Darwinism, Wallace, **93**
- 2. Ethics, Huxley, **95**
- 3. Beyond Good and Evil, Neitzsche, **96**

    B. LAW, **98**
- 4. Holy Alliance—1815, **98**
- 5. Carlsbad Decrees—1819, **99**
- 6. Revolutions of 1848, Schurz, **100**
- 7. Revolutions of 1848, British Press, **101**
- 8. Communist Manifesto, Marx, **102**
- 9. Universal Suffrage, Bismarck, **103**

    C. SOCIETY, **104**
- 10. Conditions of the Working Class, 1820s-30s. **104**
- 11. Sanitary Conditions, 1830s-40s, **104**
- 12. Master-Serf Relations—Russia, **106**

    D. ECONOMICS, **107**
- 13. Origins of Capitalism, Marx, **107**
- 14. The Industrial Revolution, Toynbee, **108**
- 15. Sir Titus Oates—Businessman, **111**
- 16. Gospel of Wealth, Carnegie, **112**

    E. SOURCES FOR PART V, **114**

VI. Contemporary Civilization, 115

    A. ETHICS, **115**
- 1. Adolph Hitler: Nazi God, **115**
- 2. Communist Ethics, Lenin, **116**

B. LAW, **117**
- 3. Wilson's Fourteen Points—1918, **117**
- 4. Program of the NSDAP—1920, **119**
- 5. A Bill of Rights, USSR—1936, **120**
- 6. The "Four Freedoms" of Roosevelt—1941, **121**
- 7. A Bill of Rights, United Nations—1948, **122**

C. SOCIETY, **122**
- 8. Soviet Justice—1930s, **122**
- 9. Herbert Tempest: An Uncommon Common Man, **124**

D. ECONOMICS, **131**
- 10. The Making of Economic Society, Heilbroner, **131**

E. SOURCES FOR PART VI, **134**

PREFACE

There are certain traditional approaches to a book of historical readings. One is to take the broad sweep of the significant sources of our history and present them from the beginning to the end. A second way is to have selections just on a single subject, such as philosophy. The problem with the first method is that, except for chronology, there is little to tie the readings together. With the second, a series of texts is needed to cover the development of mankind.

We have attempted to break with traditional organization by combining both chronology and subject. A glance at the table of contents will demonstrate that we have organized our selections around certain themes: Ethics, Law, Society, and Economics. Also the reader is divided into the traditional eras of mankind: Ancient (up to 500 C.E.); Medieval (500-1300); Renaissance (1300-1650); Enlightenment (1650-1815); Modern (1815-1914); Contemporary (since 1914). What is your approach to history? Topical or timewise? With this text you have your choice.

Finally, a word of thanks to our fellow instructors who have made comments and suggestions, particularly, Professors William Holly and Richard Clark.

I
ANCIENT CIVILIZATION

A. ETHICS

1. Akkadian Creation Epic

Early man was concerned with his origins and sought explanations for his presence on earth. The earliest indication of this concern is the creation epic of early Mesopotamia which goes back at least to ancient Babylon of two thousand years before the Christian era. This epic tells of the bringing of order out of chaos by the hero Marduk who was also the chief god of the Babylonian pantheon.

Tablet I

When on high, heaven was not named,
Below, dry land was not named.
Apsu, their first begetter,
Mummu (and) Tiamat, the mother of all of them,
Their waters combined together.
Field was not marked off, sprout had not come.
When none of the gods had yet come forth,
Had not borne a name,
No destinies had been fixed;
Then gods were created in the midst of heaven.
Lakhmu and Lakhamu came forth
Ages increased. . . .
Anshar and Kishar were created.
After many days had passed by there came forth. . . .
Anu, their son. . . .

[The river god Apsu then decided to exterminate his noisy offspring. However, Apsu was himself killed by the god Ea. This action enraged Tiamat who planned to avenge her consort and kill the gods. Informed of this by Ea, the gods met and selected Marduk as their champion again Tiamat.]

"(Oh my father), may the words of thy lips not be taken back,
May I go and accomplish the desire of thy heart'."

"Oh, my son, full of all knowledge,
Quiet Tiamat with thy supreme incantation;
Quickly proceed (on thy way)!
Thy blood will not be poured out, thou shalt surely return."
The lord rejoiced at the word of his father,
His heart exulted and he spoke to his father.
"Oh Lord of the gods, (who fixes) the fate of the great gods,
If I become thy avenger,
Conquering Tiamat, and giving life to thee,
Call an assembly and proclaim the preeminence of my lot!
That when in Upshukkinaku thou joyfully seatest thyself,
My command in place of thine should fix fates.
What I do should be unaltered,
The word of my lips be never changed or annulled."

Tablet III

Then they gathered and went,
The great gods, all of them, who fix fates,
Came into the presence of Anshar, they filled (the assembly hall),
Embracing one another in the assembly (hall),
They prepared themselves to feast at the banquet.
They ate bread, they mixed the wine,
The sweet mead confused (their senses).
Drunk, their bodies filled with drink,
They shouted aloud, with their spirits exalted,
For Marduk, their avenger, they fixed the destiny.

Tablet IV

They prepared for him a royal chamber,
In the presence of his fathers as ruler he stood.
"Thou art the weightiest among the great Thy (power of decreeing) fate is unrivalled, thy command is (like that of) Anu.
Oh Marduk, thou art mightiest among the great gods!
Thy power of decreeing fate unrivalled, thy word is like that of Anu!
From now on thy decree will not be altered,
Thine it shall be to raise up and to bring low,
Thy utterance be established, against thy command no rebellion!
None among the gods will transgress the limit (set by thee).
Abundance is pleasing to the shrines of the gods,
The place of their worship will be established as thy place.
Oh Marduk, thou art our avenger!
We give thee kingship over the entire universe,
Take thy seat in the assembly, thy word be exalted;

Thy weapon be not overcome, may it crush thy enemies.
Oh lord, the life of him who trusts in thee will be spared,
But pour out the life of the god who has planned evil." . . .
He sent forth the winds which he had created, the seven of them;
To trouble the spirit of Tiamat, they followed behind them.
Then the lord raised on high the Deluge, his mighty weapon.
He mounted the storm chariot, unequalled in power,
He harnessed and attached to it four horses,
Merciless, overwhelming, swiftly flying.
(Sharp of) teeth, bearing poison. . . .
And against Tiamat, who was foaming with wrath, thus sent forth (his answer).
"Great art thou! Thou hast exalted thyself greatly.
Thy heart hath prompted thee to arrange for battle. . . .
Thou hast (exalted) Kingu to be thy husband,
(Thou hast given him power to issue) the decrees of Anu.
(Against the gods, my fathers), thou hast planned evil,
Against the gods, my fathers, thou hast planned evil.
Let thy army be equipped, thy weapons be girded on;
Stand; I and thou, let us join in battle."
When Tiamat heard this,
She was beside herself, she lost her reason.
Tiamat shouted in a paroxysm of fury,
Trembling to the root, shaking in her foundations.
She uttered an incantation, she pronounced a magic formula.
The gods of battle, appeal to their weapons.
Then stepped forth Tiamat and the leader of the gods, Marduk.
To the fight they advanced, to the battle they drew nigh.
The lord spread his net and encompassed her,
The evil wind stationed behind him he drove into her face.
Tiamat opened her mouth to its full extent.
He drove in the evil wind before she could close her lips.
The terrible winds filled her belly,
Her heart was seized, and she held her mouth wide open.
He drove in the spear and burst open her belly,
Cutting into her entrails, he slit her heart.
He overcame her and destroyed her life;
He cast down her carcass and stood upon it.
When he had thus subjected Tiamat, the leader,
Her host was scattered, her assembly was dissolved;
And the lord trampled under foot the foundation of Tiamat.
With his merciless weapon he smashed her skull,
He cut the channels of her blood,
And made the north wind carry them to secret places.
His fathers beheld and rejoiced exceeding glad,

Presents and gifts they brought to him.
Then the lord rested and looked at the carcass.
He divided the flesh of the monster, and created marvellous things.
He split her like a fish flattened into two halves;
One half he took and made it a covering for heaven.
He drew a bolt, he stationed a watchman,.
Enjoining that the waters be not permitted to flow out.
He passed over the heavens, inspecting the regions (thereof),
And over against the Apsu, he set the dwelling of Nudimmud.
The lord measured the structure of the Deep.
He established E-sharra as a palace corresponding to it.
The palace E-sharra which he created as heaven,
He caused Anu, Enlil and Ea to inhabit their districts.

Tablet V

He made stations for the great gods,
The stars, their counterparts, the twin stars he fixed.
He fixed the year and divided it into divisions.
For the twelve months he fixed three stars.
Also for the days of the year (he had fashioned) pictures. . . .

Tablet VI

Upon (Marduk's) hearing the word of the gods,
His heart led him to create (marvellous things)
He opened his mouth and (spoke) to Ea
(What) he had conceived in his heart he imparted to him;
"My blood I will take and bone I will (form).
I will set up man that man. . . .
I will create man to inhabit (the earth),
That the worship of the gods be fixed, that they may have shrines.
But I will alter the ways of the gods, I will change. . . .
They shall be joined in concert, unto evil shall they.". . .
Ea answered him and spoke.

2. Creation According to Genesis

Attributed to the authorship of Moses, the book of Genesis presents the monotheistic account of creation which is still basic to the Judeo-Christian tradition.

In the beginning God created the heaven and the earth. And the earth was without form, and void; and darkness was upon the face of the deep. And the Spirit of God moved upon the face of the waters. And God said, "Let there be light"; and there was light. And God saw the light, that it was good and God divided the light from the darkness. And God called the light Day, and the darkness he called Night. And the evening and the morning were the first day.

And God said, "Let there be a firmament

in the midst of the waters, and let it divide the waters from the waters." And God made the firmament, and divided the waters which were under the firmament from the waters which were above the firmament: and it was so. And God called the firmament Heaven. And the evening and the morning were the second day.

And God said, "Let the waters under the heaven be gathered together unto one place, and let the dry land appear": and it was so. And God called the dry land Earth; and the gathering together of the waters called he Seas: and God saw that it was good. And God said,"Let the earth bring forth grass, the herb yielding seed, and the fruit tree yielding fruit after his kind, whose seed is in itself, upon the earth": and it was so. And the earth brought forth grass, and herb yielding seed after his kind, and the tree yielding fruit, whose seed was in itself, after his kind: and God saw that it was good. And the evening and the morning were the third day.

And God said, "Let there be lights in the firmament of the heaven to divide the day from the night; and let them be for signs, and for reasons, and for days, and years: and let them be for lights in the firmament of the heaven to give light upon the earth": and it was so. And God made two great lights; the greater light to rule the day, and the lesser light to rule the night: he made the stars also. And God set them in the firmament of the heaven to give light upon the earth. And to rule over the day and over the night, and to divide the light from the darkness: and God saw that it was good. And the evening and the morning were the fourth day.

And God said, "let the waters bring forth abundantly the moving creature that hath life, and fowl that may fly above the earth in the open firmament of heaven." And God created great whales, and every living creature that moveth, which the water brought forth abundantly, after their kind, and every winged fowl after his kind: and God saw that it was good. And God blessed them, saying, "Be fruitful, and multiply, and fill the waters in the seas, and let fowl multiply in the earth." And the evening and the morning were the fifth day.

And God said, "Let the earth bring forth the living creature after his kind, cattle and creeping thing, and beast of the earth after his kind": and it was so. And God made the beast of the earth after his kind, and cattle after their kind, and every thing that creepeth upon the earth after his kind: and God saw that it was good.

And God said, "Let us make man in our image, after our likeness: and let them have dominion over the fish of the sea, and over the fowl of the air, and over the cattle, and over all the earth, and over every creeping thing that creepeth upon the earth." So God created man in his own image, in the image of God created he him: male and female created he them. And God blessed them, and God said unto them, "Be fruitful, and multiply, and replenish the earth, and subdue it: and have dominion over the fish of the sea, and over the fowl of the air, and over every living thing that moveth upon the earth."

And God said, "Behold, I have given you every herb bearing seed, which is upon the face of all the earth, and every tree, in the which is the fruit of a tree yielding seed; to you it shall be for meat. And to every beast of the earth, and to every fowl of the air, and to every thing that creepeth upon the earth, wherein there is life, I have given every green herb for meat": and it was so. And God saw everything that he had made, and, behold, it was very good. And the evening and the morning were the sixth day.

Thus the heavens and the earth were

finished, and all the host of them. And on the seventh day God ended his work which he had made; and he rested on the seventh day from all his work which he had made. And God blessed the seventh day, and sanctified it: because that in it he had rested from all his work which God created and made.

These are the generations of the heavens and of the earth when they were created, in the day that the Lord God made the earth and the heavens. And every plant of the field before it was in the earth, and every herb of the field before it grew: for the Lord God had not caused it to rain upon the earth, and there was not a man to till the ground. But there went up a mist from the earth, and watered the whole face of the ground. And the Lord God formed man of the dust of the ground, and breathed into his nostrils the breath of life; and man became a living soul.

And the Lord God planted a garden eastward in Eden; and there he put the man whom he had formed. And out of the ground made the Lord God to grow every tree that is pleasant to the sight, and good for food; the tree of life also in the midst of the garden, and the tree of knowledge of good and evil. And a river went out of Eden to water a garden; and from thence it was parted, and became into four heads. The name of the first is Pison: that is it which compasseth the whole land of Havilah, where there is gold; and the gold of that land is good: there is bdellium and the onyx stone. And the name of the second river is Gihon: the same is it that compasseth the whole land of Ethiopia. And the name of the third river is Hiddekel: that is it which goeth toward the east of Assyria. And the fourth river is Euphrates. And the Lord God took the man, and put him into the garden of Eden to dress it and to keep it. And the Lord God commanded the man, saying, "Of every tree of the garden thou mayest freely eat: But of the tree of the knowledge of good and evil, thou shalt not eat of it: for in the day that thou eatest thereof thou shalt surely die."

And the Lord God said, "It is not good that the man should be alone; I will make an help mate for him." And out of the ground the Lord God formed every beast of the field, and every fowl of the air; and brought them unto Adam to see what he would call them: and whatsoever Adam called every living creature, that was the name thereof. And Adam gave names to all cattle, and to the fowl of the air, and to every beast of the field; but for Adam there was not found an help mate for him. And the Lord God caused a deep sleep to fall upon Adam, and he slept: and he took one of his ribs, and closed up the flesh instead thereof. And the rib, which the Lord God had taken from man made he a woman, and brought her unto the man. And Adam said, "This is now bone of my bones, and flesh of my flesh: she shall be called Woman, because she was taken out of Man. Therefore shall a man leave his father and his mother, and shall cleave unto his wife: and they shall be one flesh." And they were both naked, the man and his wife, and were not ashamed.

3. Hesiod's Creation Epic

The following selection taken from the **Theogony** *a basic work of Greek mythology, was composed in the 8th century B.C. by the writer Hesiod and reflects the thinking of the ancient Greeks on the question of creation. This work also influenced the thinking of the later Greeks and Romans. The student is now in a position to compare three creations epics with regard to* *similarities and differences and also to consider the question of the possible influence of the Ancient Near East on later peoples and cultures.*

Verily at the first Chaos came to be but next wide-bosomed Earth, the ever-sure foundation of all the deathless ones who hold the peaks of snowy Olympus, and dim Tartarus in the depth of the widepathed Earth, and Eros (Love), fairest among the deathless gods, who unnerves the limbs and overcomes the mind and wise counsels of all gods and all men within them. From Chaos came forth Erebus and black Night; but of Night were born Aether and Day, whom she conceived and bare from union in love with Erebus. And Earth first bare starry Heaven, equal to herself, to cover her on every side, and to be an ever-sure abiding-place for the blessed gods. And she brought forth long Hills, graceful haunts of the goddess-Nymphs who dwell amongst the glens of the hills. She bare also the fruitless deep with his raging swell, Pontus, without sweet union of love. But afterwards she lay with Heaven and bare deep-swirling Oceanus, Coeus and Crius and Hyperion and Iapetus, Theia and Rhea, Themis and Mnemosyne and gold-crowned Phoebe and lovely Tethys. After them was born Cronos the wily, youngest and most terrible of her children, and he hated his lusty sire.

And again, three other sons were born of Earth and Heaven, great and doughty beyond telling, Cottus and Briareos and Gyes, presumptuous children. From their shoulders sprang an hundred arms, not to be approached, and each had fifty heads upon his shoulders on their strong limbs, and irresistible was the stubborn strength that was in their great forms. For of all the children that were born of Earth and Heaven, these were the most terrible, and they were hated by their own father from the first. And he used to hide them all away in a secret place of Earth so soon as each was born, and would not suffer them to come up into the light: and Heaven rejoiced in his evil doing. But vast Earth groaned within, being straitened, and she thought a crafty and an evil wile. Forthwith she made the element of grey flint and shaped a great sickle, and told her plan to her dear sons. And she spoke, cheering them, while she was vexed in her dear heart:

"My children, gotten of a sinful father, if you will obey me, we should punish the vile outrage of your father; for he first thought of doing shameful things."

So she said; but fear seized them all, and none of them uttered a word. But great Cronos the wily took courage and answered his dear mother:

"Mother, I will undertake to do this deed, for I reverence not our father of evil name, for the first thought of doing shameful things."

So he said, and vast Earth rejoiced greatly in spirit, and set and hid him in an ambush, and put in his hands a jagged sickle, and revealed to him the whole plot.

And Heaven came, bringing on night and longing for love, and he lay about Earth spreading himself full upon her. Then the son from his ambush stretched forth his left hand and in his right took the great long sickle with jagged teeth, and swiftly lopped off his own father's members and cast them away to fall behind him. And not vainly did they fall from his hand; for all the bloody drops that gushed forth Earth received, and as the seasons moved round she bare the strong Erinyes and the great Giants with gleaming armour, holding long spears in their hands, and the Nymphs whom they call Meliae all over the boundless earth. And so soon as he had cut on the members with flint and cast them from the land into the surging sea, they were swept away over the main a long time: and a white foam spread around them from the immortal flesh, and in it there grew a maiden. First she drew near holy Cythera, and from there, afterwards, she came to sea-girt Cyprus, and came forth an awful and lovely goddess, and grass grew up about her beneath her shapely feet. Her gods and men call Aphrodite, and the foam-born goddess and rich-crowned Cytherea, because she grew amid the foam, and Cytherea because she reached Cythera, and Cyprogenes because she was born in billowy Cyprus, and Philommedes because she sprang from the members. And with her went Eros, and comely Desire followed her at her birth at the first and she went into the assembly of the gods. This honour she has from the beginning, and this is the portion allotted to her amongst men and undying gods—the whisperings of maidens and smiles and deceits with sweet delight and love and graciousness.

But these sons whom he begot himself great Heaven used to call Titans (Strainers) in reproach, for he said that they strained and did presumptuously a fearful deed, and that vengeance for it would come afterwards.

And night bare hateful Doom and black Fate and Death, and she bare Sleep and the tribe of Dreams. And again the goddess murky Night, though she lay with none, bare Blame and painful Woe, and the Hesperides who guard the rich, golden apples and the trees bearing fruit beyond glorious Ocean. Also she bare the Destinies and ruthless avenging Fates, Clotho and Lachesis and Atropos, who give men at their birth both evil and good to have, and they pursue the transgressions of men and of gods: and these goddesses never cease from their dread anger until they punish the sinner with a sore penalty. Also deadly Night bare Nemesis (Indignation) to afflict mortal men, and after her, deceit and Friendship and hateful Age and hard-hearted Strife.

4. Stoicism of Marcus Aurelius

Marcus Aurelius (161-180 A.D.) the last of the "Good Emperors" epitomizes the Platonic ideal of the philosopher king. The **Thoughts** *or* **Meditations** *from which this reading was taken, was written as a private diary recording the most intimate thoughts of a stoic philosopher.*

Every morning repeat to thyself: I shall meet with a busybody, an ingrate, and a bully; with treachery, envy, and selfishness. All these vices have fallen to their share because they know not good and evil. But I have contemplated the nature of the good and seen that it is the beautiful; of evil, and seen that it is deformity; of the sinner, and seen that it is kindred to my own—kindred, not because he shares the same flesh and blood and is sprung from the same seed, but because he partakes of the same reason and the same spark of divinity. How then can any of these harm me? For none can involve me in the shameful save myself. Or how can I be angered with my kith and kin, or cherish hatred towards them?

For we are all created to work together, as the members of one body—feet, hands, and eyelids, or the upper and nether teeth. Whence, to work against each other is contrary to nature;—but this is the very essence of anger and aversion.

This thing that I call "myself" is compact of flesh, breath, and reason. Thou art even now in the throes of death; despise therefore the flesh. It is but a little blood, a few bones, a paltry net woven from nerves and veins and arteries. Consider next thy breath. What a trifle it is! A little air, and this for ever changing: every minute of every hour we are gasping it forth and sucking it in again!

The works of God are full of providence; the works of Fortune are not independent of Nature, but intertwisted and interwined with those directed by providence. Thence flow all things. Co-factors, too, are necessity and the common welfare of the whole universe whereof thou art part. Now whatever arises from the nature of the whole, and tends to its well-being, is good also for every part of that nature. But the well-being of the universe depends on change, not merely of the elementary, but also of the compound. Let these dogmas suffice thee, if dogmas thou must have; but put off that thirst for books, and see thou die of good cheer, not with murmurs on thy lips, but blessing God truthfully and with all thy heart.

Bethink thee how long thou hast delayed to do these things; how many days of grace heaven hath vouchsafed thee and thou neglected. Now is the time to learn at last what is the nature of the universe whereof thou art part; what of the power that governs the universe, whereof thou art an emanation. Forget not there is a boundary set to thy time, and that if thou use it not to uncloud thy soul it will anon be gone, and thou with it, never to return again.

Let it be thy hourly care to do stoutly what thy hand findeth to do, as becomes a man and a Roman, with carefulness, unaffected dignity, humanity, freedom, and justice. Free thyself from the obsession of all other thoughts; for free thyself thou wilt, if thou but perform every action as though it were the last of thy life, without light-mindedness, with swerving through force of passion from the dictates of reason, without hypocrisy, without self-love, without chafing at destiny.

Thou seest how few things are needful for man to live a happy and godlike life: for, if he observe these, heaven will demand no more.

God views the minds of all men in their nakedness, stripped of the casings and husks and impurities of the material. For, solely in virtue of the intellectual part of Himself, He touches directly the human intellect that emanates from Him and has flowed into these bodies of ours. So train thou thyself to do likewise, and thou shalt be quit of this sore distraction of thine. For he who has no eyes for our fleshly covering surely will not trouble himself with the contemplation of a man's house, raiment, fame, or aught else of these outer trappings and stage decorations!

There are three things whereof thou art compound: body, breath, and mind. Of these the first two are thine in so far as it is thy duty to assume their stewardship; but the third alone is thine absolutely. Wherefore, if thou wilt put away from thyself and thy mind all that others do or say, all thou thyself hast said or done, all disturbing thoughts of the future, all the vicissitudes of thy fleshly garment and its conjunct breath, with all that the circumfluent vortex whirls along, so that the intellective power, exempt and purified from the things of destiny, may dwell free and master in its own household, practicing justice of action, resigned to all that chances, and speaking the truth,—if, I say "thou wilt put aside from this reason of thine all accretions born of the fleshly affections, all time to come, and all time past, likening thyself to the Empedoclean globe— that perfect sphere rejoicing with great joy in its stability,"—and striving to live only the life thou livest, in other words the present, then the power will be thine to pass the span that is left between thee and death in calmness and cheerfulness and content with the godhead that resides within thee.

I have often marvelled how it is that every

one loves himself more than the rest of human kind, yet values his own opinion of himself less than that of others. At all events, were some god or some sage to stand by a man and bid him entertain no idea, no thought, within himself without simultaneously uttering it aloud, he could not abide the ordeal for a single day. So true it is that we have more respect for our neighbours and their thoughts of us than we have for ourselves!

B. LAW

5. Code of Hammurabi

As the first three selections demonstrate, early man saw a divine hand in creation. Early laws were similar. Although not man's first set of "rules," Hammurabi's Code is the earliest and most complete laws known. Two aspects of the Code are interesting: its class distinctions—compare numbers 196 and 197 to 198; and sex discrimination—number 129.

1. If a man has accused another of laying a death spell upon him, but has not proved it, he shall be put to death.

3. If a man has borne false witness in a trial, or has not established the statement that he has made, if that case be a capital trial, that man shall be put to death.

4. If he has borne false witness in a civil law case, he shall pay the damages in that suit.

5. If a judge has given a verdict, rendered a decision, granted a written judgment, and afterward has altered his judgment, that judge shall be prosecuted for altering the judgment he gave and shall pay twelvefold the penalty laid down in that judgment. Further, he shall be publicly expelled from his judgment-seat and shall not return nor take his seat with the judges at a trial.

6. If a man has stolen goods from a temple, or house, he shall be put to death; and he that has received the stolen property from him shall be put to death.

25. If a fire has broken out in a man's house and one who has come to put it out has coveted the property of the householder and appropriated any of it, that man shall be cast into the selfsame fire.

53, 54. If a man has neglected to strengthen his dike and has not kept his dike strong, and a breach has broken out in his dike, and the waters have flooded the meadow, the man in whose dike the breach has broken out shall restore the corn he has caused to be lost. [54.] If he be not able to restore the corn, he and his goods shall be sold, and the owners of the meadow whose corn the water has carried away shall share the money.

55. If a man has opened his runnel for watering and has left it open, and the water has flooded his neighbor's field, he shall pay him an average crop.

128. If a man has a wife and has not executed a marriage contract, that woman is not a wife.

129. If a man's wife be caught lying with another, they shall be strangled and cast into the water. If the wife's husband would save his wife, the king can save his servant.

130. If a man has ravished another's betrothed wife, who is a virgin, while still living in her father's house, and has been caught in the act, that man shall be put to death; the woman shall go free.

131. If a man's wife has been accused by

her husband, and has not been caught lying with another, she shall swear her innocence, and return to her house.

132. If a man's wife has the finger pointed at her on account of another, but has not been lying with him, for her husband's sake she shall plunge into the sacred river.

195. If a son has struck his father, his hands shall be cut off.

196. If a man has knocked out the eye of a patrician, his eye shall be knocked out.

187. If he has broken the limb of a patrician, his limb shall be broken.

198. If he has knocked out the eye of a plebeian or has broken the limb of a plebeian, he shall pay one mina of silver.

199. If he has knocked out the eye of a patrician's servant, or broken the limb of a patrician's servant, he shall pay half his value.

200. If a patrician has knocked out the tooth of a man that is his equal, his tooth shall be knocked out.

201. If he has knocked out the tooth of a plebeian, he shall pay one-third of a mina of silver.

202. If a man has smitten the privates of a man, higher in rank than he, he shall be scourged with sixty blows of an ox-hide scourge, in the assembly.

203. If a man has smitten the privates of a patrician of his own rank, he shall pay one mina of silver.

209. If a man has struck a free woman with child, and has caused her to miscarry, he shall pay ten shekels for her miscarriage.

210. If that woman die, his daughter shall be killed.

211. If it be the daughter of a plebeian, that has miscarried through his blows, he shall pay five shekels of silver.

212. If that woman die, he shall pay half a mina of silver.

213. If he has struck a man's maid and caused her to miscarry, he shall pay two shekels of silver.

214. If that woman die, he shall pay one-third of a mina of silver.

6. The Ten Commandments

"And God spoke all these words," begins the ten basic rules of morality of the Judeo-Christian religions. Unlike earlier codes the Commandments and the Mosiac Law for the first time recognized all people equal before the law.

And God spoke all these words, saying: I am the Lord your God, which has brought you out of the land of Egypt, out of the house of bondage.

You shall have no other gods before me.

You shall not make for yourself any graven image, or any likeness of any thing that is in heaven above, or that is in the earth beneath, or that is in the water under the earth.

You shall not bow yourself down to them, nor serve them: for I the Lord your God am a jealous God, visiting the iniquity of the fathers upon the children unto the third and fourth generation of those that hate me; and showing mercy unto thousands of those that love me and keep my commandments.

You shall not take the name of the Lord your God in vain: for the Lord will not hold him guiltless that takes his name in vain.

Remember the sabbath day, to keep it holy. Six days shall you labor and do all your work, but the seventh day is the sabbath of the Lord your God: in it you shall not do any work, you nor your son, nor your daughter, nor your manservant, nor your maidservant, nor your cattle, nor the stranger that is within your gates. For in six days the Lord made heaven and earth, the sea, and all that in them is, and rested the seventh day: wherefore the Lord blessed the sabbath day, and hallowed it.

Honor your father and your mother: that your days may be long upon the land which the Lord your God gives you.

You shall not kill.

You shall not commit adultery.

You shall not steal.

You shall not bear false witness against your neighbor.

You shall not covet your neighbor's house, you shall not covet your neighbor's wife, nor his manservant, nor his maidservant, nor his ox, nor his ass, nor anything that is your neighbor's.

7. Spartan Constitution, Plutarch

Laws, to the Greeks, were man-made, not divine creations. The two great states of Ancient Greece created two uniquely different systems. In Sparta the semimythical Lycurgus created an oligarchy which controlled the lives of its Spartan citizens from birth to death.

Amongst the many changes and alterations which Lycurgus made, the first and of the greatest importance was the establishment of the senate, which . . . gave steadiness and safety to the commonwealth . . . like ballast in a ship, which always kept things in a just equilibrium; the twenty-eight always adhering to the kings so far as to resist democracy, and, on the other hand, supporting the people against the establishment of absolute monarchy. . . .

After the creation of the thirty senators, his next task, and, indeed, the most hazardous he ever undertook, was the making of a new division of their lands. For there was an extreme inequality amongst them, and their state was overloaded with a multitude of indigent and necessitous persons, while its whole wealth had centered upon a very few. To the end, therefore, that he might expel from the state arrogance and envy, luxury and crime, and those yet more inveterate diseases of want and superfluity, he obtained of them to renounce their properties, and to consent to a new division of the land, and that they should live all together on an equal footing; merit to be their only road to eminence, and the disgrace of evil, and credit of worthy acts, their one measure of difference between man and man.

Upon their consent to these proposals . . . he divided the country of Laconia in general into thirty thousand equal shares, and the part attached to the city of Sparta into nine thousand; these he distributed . . . . A lot was so much as to yield, one year with another, about seventy bushels of grain for the master of the family, and twelve for his wife, with a suitable proportion of oil and wine. And this he thought sufficient to keep their bodies in good health and strength; superfluities they were better without. . . .

In the next place, he declared an outlawry of all needless and superfluous arts; but here he might almost have spared his proclamation; for they of themselves would have gone after the gold and silver, the money which remained being not so proper payment for curious work; for, being of iron, it was scarcely portable, neither, if they should take the pains to export it, would it pass amongst the other Greeks, who ridiculed it. So there was now no more means of purchasing foreign goods and small wares; merchants sent no shiploads into Laconian ports; no rhetorc-master, no itinerant fortuneteller, no harlot-monger, or gold or silversmith, engraver, or jeweler, set foot in a country which had no money; so that luxury, deprived little by little of that which fed and fomented it, wasted to nothing, and died away of itself. For the rich had no advantage here over the poor, as their wealth and abundance had no road to come abroad by, but were shut up at home doing nothing. And in this way they became excellent artists in common, necessary things; bedsteads, chairs, and tables, and suchlike staple utensils in a family, were admirably well made there; their cup, particularly, was very much in fashion, and eagerly bought up by soldiers, as Critias reports; for its color was such as to prevent water, drunk upon necessity and disagreeable to look at, from being noticed; and the shape of it was such that the mud stuck to the sides, so that only the purer part came to the drinker's mouth. For this, also, they had to thank their lawgiver, who, by relieving the artisans of the trouble of making useless things, set them to show their skill in giving beauty to those of daily and indispensable use.

The third and most masterly stroke of this great lawgiver, by which he struck a yet more effectual blow against luxury and the desire of riches, was the ordinance he made, that they should all eat in common, of the same bread and same meat, and of kinds that were specified, and should not spend their lives at home, laid on costly couches at splendid tables, delivering themselves up into the hands of their tradesmen and cooks, to fatten them in corners, like greedy brutes, and to ruin not their minds only but their very bodies, which, enfeebled by indulgence and excess, would stand in need of long sleep, warm bathing, freedom from work, and, in a word, of as much care and attention as if they were continually sick. . . . For the rich, being obliged to go to the same table with the poor, could not make use of or enjoy their abundance, nor so much as please their vanity by looking at or displaying it. . . .

Lycurgus would never reduce his laws into writing; nay, there is a Rhetra expressly to forbid it. For he thought that the most material points, and such as most directly tended to the public welfare, being imprinted on the hearts of their youth by a good discipline, would be sure to remain, and would find a stronger security, than any compulsion would be.

8. Athenian Democracy, Pericles

Unlike the Spartan Constitution, Pericles takes pride in the "equal opportunity" of all Athenian citizens to partake in ruling Athens. But what Pericles does not mention is the narrow application of "citizen." No female, slave, freedman, or foreign-born could ever receive that honor.

Our form of government does not enter into rivalry with the institutions of others. We do not copy our neighbors, but are an example to them. It is true that we are called a democracy, for the administration is in the hands of the many and not of the few. But while the law secures equal justice to all alike in their private disputes, the claim of excellence is also recognized; and when a citizen is in any way distinguished, he is preferred to the public service, not as a matter of privilege, but as the reward of merit. Neither is poverty a bar, but a man may benefit his country whatever be the obscurity of his condition. There is no exclusiveness in our public life, and in our private intercourse we are not suspicious of one another, nor angry with our neighbor if he does what he likes; we do not put on sour looks at him which, though harmless, are not pleasant. While we are thus unconstrained in our private intercourse, a spirit of reverence pervades our public acts; we are prevented from doing wrong by respect for authority and for the laws, having an especial regard to those which are ordained for the protection of the injured as well as to those unwritten laws which bring upon the transgressor of them the reprobation of the general sentiment.

And we have not forgotten to provide for our weary spirits many relaxations from toil; we have regular games and sacrifices throughout the year; at home the style of our life is refined; and the delight which we daily feel in all these things helps to banish melancholy. Because of the greatness of our city the fruits of the whole earth flow in upon us; so that we enjoy the goods of other countries as freely as of our own.

Then, again, our military training is in many respects superior to that of our adversaries. Our city is thrown open to the world, and we never expel a foreigner or prevent him from seeing or learning anything of which the secret if revealed to an enemy might profit him. We rely not upon management or trickery, but upon our own hearts and hands. And in the matter of education, whereas they from early youth are always undergoing laborious exercises which are to make them brave, we live at ease, and yet are equally ready to face the perils which they face. . . .

For we are lovers of the beautiful, yet with economy, and we cultivate the mind without loss of manliness. Wealth we employ, not for talk and ostentation, but when there is a real use for it. To avow poverty with us is no disgrace; the true disgrace is in doing nothing to avoid it. An Athenian citizen does not neglect the state because he takes care of his own household; and even those of us who are engaged in business have a very fair idea of politics. We alone regard a man who takes no interest in public affairs, not as a harmless, but as a useless character; and if few of us are originators, we are all sound judges of a policy. The great impediment to action is, in our opinion, not discussion, but the want of that knowledge which is gained by discussion preparatory to action. For we have a peculiar power of thinking before we act and of acting too, whereas other men are courageous from ignorance but hesitate upon reflection. And they are surely to be esteemed the bravest spirits, who, having the clearest sense both of the pains and pleasures of life, do not on that account shrink from danger. In doing good, again, we are unlike others; we make our friends by conferring, not by receiving favours. Now he who confers a favour is the firmer friend, because he would fain by kindness keep alive the memory of an obligation; but the recipient is colder in his feelings, because he knows that in requiting another's generosity he will not be winning gratitude but only paying a debt. We alone do good to our neighbors not upon a calculation of interest, but in the confidence of freedom and in a frank and fearless spirit.

9. Roman Constitution, Polybius

The Romans were superior as a nation of law makers. Much of modern European law, as well as American, is based on Roman. Possibly there is also a warning to us on what happens to a republic when the system goes wrong.

As for the Roman constitution, it had three elements, each of them possessing sovereign powers: and their respective share of power in the whole state had been regulated with such a scrupulous regard to equality and equilibrium, that no one could say for certain, not even a native, whether the constitution as a whole were an aristocracy or democracy or despotism. And no wonder: for if we confine our observation to the power of the Consuls we should be inclined to regard it as despotic; if on that of the Senate, as aristocratic; and if finally one looks at the power possessed by the people it would seem a clear case of a democracy. What the exact powers of these several parts were and still, with slight modifications, are, I will now state.

The Consuls, before leading out the legions, remain in Rome and are the supreme masters of the administration. All other magistrates, except the Tribunes, are under them and take their orders. They introduce foreign ambassadors to the Senate; bring matters requiring deliberation before it; and see to the execution of the decrees. If, again, there are any matters of state which require the authorization of the people, it is their business to see to them, to summon the popular meetings, to bring the proposals before them, and to carry out the decrees of the majority. In the preparations for war also, and in a word in the entire administration of a campaign, they have all but absolute power. It is competent to them to impose on the allies such levies as they think good, to appoint the military tribunes, to make up the roll for soldiers and select those that are suitable. Besides they have absolute power of inflicting punishment on all who are under their command while on active service: and they have authority to expend as much of the public money as they choose, being accompanied by a quaestor who is entirely at their orders. A survey of these powers would in fact justify our describing the constitution as despotic, a clear case of royal government. Nor will it affect the truth of my description if any of the institutions I have described are changed in our time or in that of our posterity: and the same remarks apply to what follows.

The Senate has first of all control of the treasury, and regulates the receipts and disbursements alike. For the Quaestors cannot issue any public money for the various departments of the state without a decree of the Senate, except for the service of the Consuls. The Senate controls also what is by far the largest and most important expenditure, that, namely, which is made by the censors every *lustrum* for the repair or construction of public buildings; this money cannot be obtained by the censors except by the grant of the Senate. Similarly all crimes committed, such as treason, conspiracy, poisoning, or wilful murder, are in the hands of the Senate. Besides, if any individual or state among the Italian allies requires a controversy to be settled, a penalty to be assessed, help or protection to be afforded, all this is the province of the Senate. Or again, outside Italy, if it is necessary to send an embassy to reconcile warring communities or to remind them of their duty, or sometimes to impose requisitions upon them, or to receive their submission, or finally to proclaim war against them, this too is the business of the Senate. In like manner, the reception to be given to foreign ambassadors in Rome and the answers to be returned to them, are decided by the Senate. With such business the people have nothing to do. Consequently, if one were staying at Rome when the Consuls were not in town, one would imagine the constitution to be a complete aristocracy: and this has been the idea entertained by many Greeks, and by many kings as well, from the fact that nearly all the business they had with Rome was settled by the Senate.

After this one would naturally be inclined to ask what part is left for the people in the constitution, when the Senate has these various functions, especially the control of the receipts and expenditure of the exchequer; and when the Consuls, again, have absolute power over the details of military preparation and an absolute authority in the field? There is, however, a part left the people, and it is a most important one. For the people is the sole fountain of honor and of punishment; and it is by these two things and these alone that dynasties and constitutions and, in a word, human society are held together: for where the distinction between them is not sharply drawn both in theory and practice, there no undertaking can be properly administered, as indeed we might expect when good and bad are held in exactly the same honor. The people then are the only court to decide matters of life and death; and even in cases where the penalty is money, if the sum to be assessed is sufficiently serious, and especially when the accused have held the higher magistracies. And in regard to this arrangement there is one point deserving especial commendation and record. Men who are on trial for their lives at Rome, while sentence is in process of being voted, if even only one of the tribes whose votes are needed to ratify the sentence has not voted, have the privilege at Rome of openly departing and condemning themselves to a voluntary exile. Such men are safe at Naples, or Praeneste or at Tibur, and at other towns with which this arrangement has been duly ratified on oath.

Again, it is the people who bestow offices on the deserving, which are the most honorable rewards of virtue. It has also the absolute power of passing or repealing laws; and, most important of all, it is the people who deliberate on the question of peace or war. And when provisional terms are made for alliance, suspension of hostilities, or treaties, it is the people who ratify them or the reverse.

C. SOCIETY

10. Egyptian Social Customs, Herodotus

This reading comes from the Fifth Century, B.C. **Histories** *by the Ancient Greek Herodotus. Herodotus, who is known as the Father of History, pointed out how Egyptian social customs differed from those of other Ancient peoples. How and why did the Egyptians come to develop such unique customs?*

Not only is the climate [of Egypt] different from that of the rest of the world, and the rivers unlike any other rivers, but the people also, in most of their manners and customs, exactly reverse the common practice of mankind. The women attend the markets and trade, while the men sit at home at the loom; and here, while the rest of the world works the woof up the warp, the Egyptians work it down; the women likewise carry burdens upon their shoulders, while the men carry them upon their heads. . . . They eat their food out of doors in the streets, but relieve themselves in their houses, giving as a reason that what is unseemly, but necessary, ought to be done in secret, but what has nothing unseemly about it, should be done openly. A woman cannot serve the priestly office, eiter for god or goddess, but men are priests to both; sons need not support their parents unless they choose, but daughters must, whether they choose or no.

In other countries the priests have long hair, in Egypt their heads are shaven;

elsewhere it is customary, in mourning, for near relations to cut their hair close; the Egyptians, who wear no hair at any other time, when they lose a relative, let their beards and the hair on their heads grow long. All other men pass their lives separate from animals, the Egyptians have animals always living with them; others make barley and wheat their food, it is a disgrace to do so in Egypt. . . . Dough they knead with their feet, but they mix mud, and even take up dung with their hands. . . . Their men wear two garments apiece, their women but one. They put on the rings and fasten the ropes to sails inside, others put them outside. When they write or calculate, instead of going, like the Greeks, from left to right, they move their hand from right to left; and they insist, notwithstanding, that it is they who go to the right, and the Greeks who go to the left. They have two quite different kinds of writing, one of which is called sacred, the other common.

Embalming

The mode of embalming, according to the most perfect process, is the following: They take first a crooked piece of iron, and with it draw out the brain through the nostrils, thus getting rid of a portion, while the skull is cleared of the rest by rinsing with drugs; next they make a cut along the flank with a sharp Ethiopian stone, and take out the whole contents of the abdomen, which they then cleanse, washing it thoroughly with palm-wine, and again frequently with an infusion of pounded aromatics. After this they fill the cavity with the purest bruised myrrh, with cassia, and every other sort of spicery except frankincense, and sew up the opening. Then the body is placed in natrum for seventy days, and covered entirely over. After the expiration of that space of time, which must not be exceeded, the body is washed, and wrapped round, from head to foot, with bandages of fine linen cloth, smeared over with gum, which is used generally by the Egyptians in place of glue, and in this state it is given back to the relations, who enclose it in a wooden case which they have had made for the purpose, shaped into the figure of a man. Then fastening the case, they place it in a sepulchral chamber, upright against the wall.

11. Hazards of City Life in Rome, Juvenal

This poem by the Roman poet, Juvenal (60?-?140 A.D.) provides the reader with information on living conditions among the common people of Ancient Rome. How do the material possessions of the Roman common man compare with those of contemporary man?

"O! may I live where no such fears molest, No midnight fires burst on my hour of rest!
For here 'tis terror all; midst the loud cry
Of 'water! water' the scared neighbors fly,
With all their haste can seize, the flames aspire.
And the third floor is wrapt in smoke and fire
While you, unconscious, doze. Up, ho! and know,
The impetuous blaze which spreads dismay below,
By swift degrees will reach the aerial cell
Where crouching, underneath the tiles you dwell,
Where your tame doves their golden couplets rear,
'And you could no mischance but drowning fear!

Codrus had but one bed, and that too short
For his short wife; 'his goods of every sort
Were else but few: six little pipkins graced
His cupboard head; a little can was placed
On a snug shelf beneath, and near it lay
A Chiron [a statue of a Centaur], of the same cheap marble—clay.
And was this all? O no: he yet possest
A few Greek books, shrined in an ancient chest,
Where barbarous mice through many an inlet crept
And fed on heavenly numbers while he slept.
"Codrus, in short, had nothing too!
One curse alone was wanting to complete
His woes: that cold and hungry, through the street
The wretch should beg, and in the hour of need
Find none to lodge, to clothe him, or to feed!''

12. A Roman Banquet, Petronius

In contrast to the previous selection on the common people of Rome, Petronius Arbiter wrote of his observations and experiences among the wealthy and powerful Romans of the First century, A.D. This reading describes a banquet hosted by Trilmachio, a crass parvenu. The reader will note Trilmachio's ostentatious display and his "conspicuous consumption." Are there any parallels between Trilmachio's behavior and contemporary man?

Presently we took our places, and Alexandrian slaves poured water cooled with snow over our hands, while others approached our feet and with great skill began paring our corns; nor were they silent even over this rather disagreeable task, but kept singing all the time.

A very choice lot of hors d'oeuvres was then brought in; for we had already taken our places, all except Trimalchio himself for whom the seat of honor was reserved. Among the objects placed before us was a young ass made of Corinthian bronze and fitted with a sort of pack-saddle which contained on one side pale green olives and on the other side dark ones. Two dishes flanked this; and on the margin of them Trimalchio's name was engraved and the weight of the silver.

In the midst of all this magnificence Trimalchio was brought in to the sound of music and propped up on a pile of well-stuffed cushions. The very sight of him almost made us laugh in spite of ourselves; for his shaven pate was thrust out of a scarlet robe, and around his neck he had tucked a long fringed napkin with a broad purple stripe running down the middle of it. On the little finger of his left hand he wore a huge gilt ring, and on the last joint of the next finger a ring that appeared to be of solid gold, but having little iron stars upon it. Moreover, he had bared his right arm, which was adorned with a golden bracelet and an ivory circle fastened by a glittering clasp.

As he sat there picking his teeth with a silver toothpick . . . a tray was brought in with a basket on which a wooden fowl was placed with its wings spread out in a circle after the fashion of setting hens. Immediately two slaves approached and amid a burst of music began to poke around in the straw, and having presently discovered there some pea-hens' eggs, they distributed them among the guests.

Trimalchio looked up during this operation and said, "Gentlemen, I had the hens' eggs placed under this fowl; but I'm rather afraid they have young chickens in them. Let's see whether they're still fit to suck."

So we took our spoons, which weighed not less than a half a pound each, and broke the egg-shells, which were made of flour paste. As I did so, I was almost tempted to throw my egg on the floor, for it looked as though a chicken had just been formed inside; but when I heard an old diner-out by my side saying: "There's bound to be something good here," I thrust my finger through the shell and drew out a plump reed-bird, surrounded by yolk of egg well seasoned with pepper.

Trimalchio . . . called for the . . . dainties, inviting us with a loud voice to take a drink of honeyed wine also. Just then, however, at a signal given by music, all the dishes were swept off at once by a troop of slaves who sang over their work. Amid the bustle, a silver dish happened to fall on the floor, and when one of the servants started to pick it up, Trimalchio ordered him to be soundly cuffed, and told him to throw it down again; and presently there came in a servant, broom in hand, who swept up the silver dish along with the rest of the rubbish that lay on the floor. After this, there entered two long-haired Ethiopian slaves carrying little bags such as are used for sprinkling the sand in the amphitheatre, and from these they poured wine over our hands; for water was not good enough to wash in at that house.

A troupe [of Homeric actors] . . . came in, clattering their shields and spears. Trimalchio sat up on his couch, and the Homeric actors in a pompous fashion began a dialogue in Greek verse.

The Homeric actors set up a shout, and while the slaves bustled about, a boiled calf was brought in on an enormous dish and with a helmet placed upon it. The actor who took the part of Ajax followed with a drawn sword, fell upon it as though he were mad, and hacking this way and that he cut up the calf and offered the bits to us on the point of his sword, to our great surprise.

We had no time to admire these elegant proceedings, for all of a sudden the ceiling of the room began to rumble and the whole dining-room shook. In consternation I jumped up, fearing lest some acrobat should come down through the roof; and all the other guests in surprise looked upward as though they expected some miracle from heaven. But, lo and behold, the panels of the ceiling slid apart, and suddenly a great hoop as though shaken off from a hogshead was let down, having gold crowns with jars of perfume hanging about its entire circumference. These things we were invited to accept as keepsakes, and presently a tray was set before us full of cakes with an image of Priapus as a centre piece made of confectionery and holding in its generous bosom apples of every sort and grapes, in the usual fashion, as being the god of gardens. We eagerly snatched at this magnificent display, and suddenly renewed our mirth at discovering a novel trick: for all the cakes and all the apples, when pressed the least bit, squirted saffron water into our faces.

While this was going on, three slaves dressed in white tunics entered, two of whom placed images of the household gods upon the table, and the other one carrying around a bowl of wine called out "God bless us all!" Trimalchio told us that one image was the image of the God of Business, the second the image of the God of Luck, and the third the image of the God of Gain. There was a very striking bust of Trimalchio also, and as everybody else kissed it, I was ashamed not to do the same.

D. ECONOMICS

13. Economic Advantages of Athens, Xenophon

Xenophon was a noted military leader and a famous journalistic historian. His economic credentials were meager, but his intuitive impressions reveal quite a bit about the Athenian economy of long ago.

For myself I hold to the opinion that the qualities of the leading statesmen in a state, whatever they be, are reproduced in the character of the constitution itself.

As, however, it has been maintained by certain leading statesmen in Athens that the recognised standard of right and wrong is as high at Athens as elsewhere, but that, owing to the pressure of poverty on the masses, a certain measure of injustice in their dealing with the allied states could not be avoided; I set myself to discover whether by any manner of means it were possible for the citizens of Athens to be supported solely from the soil of Attica itself, which was obviously the most equitable solution. For if so, herein lay, as I believed, the antidote at once to their own poverty and to the feeling of suspicion with which they are regarded by the rest of Hellas.

I had no sooner begun my investigation than one fact presented itself clearly to my mind, which is that the country itself is made by nature to provide the amplest resources. And with a view to establishing the truth of this initial proposition I will describe the physical features of Attica.

In the first place, the extraordinary mildness of the climate is proved by the actual products of the soil. Numerous plants which in many parts of the world appear as stunted leafless growths are here fruit-bearing. And as with the soil so with the sea indenting our coasts, the varied productivity of which is exceptionally great. Again with regard to those kindly fruits of earth which Providence bestows on man season by season, one and all they commence earlier and end later in this land. Nor is the supremacy of Attica shown only in those products which year after year flourish and grow old, but the land contains treasures of a more perennial kind. Within its folds lies imbedded by nature an unstinted store of marble, out of which are chiselled temples and altars of rarest beauty and the glittering splendour of images sacred to the gods. This marble, moreover, is an object of desire to many foreigners, Hellenes and barbarians alike. Then there is land which, although it yields no fruit to the sower, needs only to be quarried in order to feed many times more mouths than it could as corn-land. Doubtless we owe it to a divine dispensation that our land is veined with silver; if we consider how many neighbouring states lie round us by land and sea and yet into none of them does a single thinnest vein of silver penetrate.

Indeed it would be scarcely irrational to maintain that the city of Athens lies at the navel, not of Hellas merely, but of the habitable world. So true is it, that the farther we remove from Athens the greater the extreme of heat or cold to be encountered; or to use another illustration, the traveller who desires to traverse the confines of Hellas from end to end will find that, whether he voyages by sea or by land, he is describing a circle, the centre of which is Athens.

Once more, this land though not literally sea-girt has all the advantages of an island, being accessible to every wind that blows, and can invite to its bosom or waft from its shore all products, since it is peninsular; whilst by land it is the emporium of many markets; as being a portion of the continent.

Lastly whilst the majority of states have barbarian neighbours, the source of many troubles, Athens has as her next-door neighbours civilised states which are themselves far remote from the barbarians.

14. Economic Decline of Rome, Ferdinand Lot

Ferdinand Lot is obviously knowledgeable in economic history. And his account of the Roman economy tells part of the story of the "decline and fall" of Rome. But beyond this story line, there are many insights about the several strengths and many weaknesses of ancient economics, including that of Rome itself.

We are now faced with a problem of the highest importance. How can we explain the fact that the Roman world, economically prosperous at the end of the Republic and during the first two centuries of the Empire, was irreparably ruined? The storm of the third century was terrible in its political consequences, and the monetary system suffered serious upheavals. But Aurelian, Diocletian and Constantine set the Roman world on its feet once more, refounded the administration, improved the financial system, and the currency again became nearly as good as in the first century. Nevertheless nothing could stop the downfall, which only became marked in the course of the fourth and the fifth centuries.

This is a very surprising phenomenon to us, who are accustomed to an ever-growing prosperity. A commercial crisis or a war may interrupt this prosperity but we are convinced that after a more or less long period of arrest, business will recover and that the production of wealth will never stop. Why do we have this conviction? Because we live under the capitalist system, under which all the forces of society are bent on the production of [goods] which are sold in wider and wider markets.

Was it the same with Antiquity? In other words, had Antiquity any knowledge of a real capitalist system? . . .

Let us see whether at Rome capital was "invested," as is asserted, in industry and commerce, in which case the existence of capitalism could not be called in question.

Capital and Industry

From a very early period of Roman history, the crafts became freed from the household, or from domestic economy, to be at the service of the public. Specialization in the crafts and the division of labour were far advanced from the third and second centuries B.C. onwards. Crafts and trades, sometimes organized into "colleges," tended to gather in particular streets. The town dweller could find bakers from whom to purchase bread, shops where fried fish was sold, inns, barbers' and clothiers' shops. But even this does not imply any industrial capitalist production. . . .

In fact capital, which was so plentiful at the end of the Republic and the beginning of the Empire, was not applied or was applied only to a small extent to industry. This already constitutes a profound and essential difference between Roman and modern or contemporary economics.

Why was no attempt made to invest money in industry?

In the first place because of the obstacle of domestic economy. The latter was deeply rooted in the prevailing habits. Every great *villa* possessed not merely its hand-mills, bakehouses, workshops for agricultural requirements (a forge, a carpenters' shop), but also workshops for weaving and clothes, entrusted to the women and slaves. The aristocracy kept embroiderers, gilders, chasers, goldsmiths, painters, architects, sculptors, hairdressers, who were either slaves or freedmen. "Rich families felt a kind of vainglory in being able to say that all the needs of the house could be satisfied by the work within the house itself; thus everything was manufactured in the house, even articles of luxury." To buy things outside was considered a kind of disgrace.

On the other hand, modern capitalism has succeeded, at least in Western Europe, in entirely breaking down domestic industry' by making use of progress in techinque. Now it is a significant fact that the technique of the crafts does not seem to have made any appreciable progress amongst the Romans.

We have here a very important special case of the phenomenon of the paralysis of invention which shows itself in all the spheres of human activity, art, literature, science and philosophy, in Greece as early as the second century B.C., in Rome in the second century A.D.

In the absence of technical improvement, capital was not required for investment in industry, while the inventive spirit, in its turn, was not stimulated by the prospect of the profits to be brought to it by capital from applying itself to the improvement of industrial technique. These reciprocal actions and reactions of the inventive spirit and of capitalism, so marked in Europe as early as the eighteenth century and even before, did not exist in the Roman world.

But in the absence of machines and improved tools, could not the employment of human hands at a low or at a minimum price, the employment of slaves, attract capital? Only for a moment. There have been some important enterprises started with slaves.

At Rome also some attempts were made. Contractors and capitalists thought they would do good business by making profits by the work of slaves trained to practise crafts. But the profits soon showed themselves very slender. In the first place money had to be spent on buying the slave, or else, if he was already in the house, on training him, teaching him his craft. If a crisis arises, the slave has still to be kept, however inadequately.

Above all, his working capacity and his yield are very inferior to those of the free man, the margin being so small that the master's profits may vanish altogether. If people kept gangs of slaves (and they did this only up to about the second century) it was from vanity and for show, rather than for any very tangible advantages. Finally, as the master wishes to use his slaves for everything, for labours of the field as well as for town crafts, he cannot carry the division of labour very far. Thus the economics of slavery are proved to be essentially anti-capitalist. . . .

Urban Market

Was Rome a market? In a certain sense it was, and even a world market as we should say, all the products of nature and art flowing there. But Rome sold nothing in return, since practically nothing was produced there. The populace, kept in semi-idleness by the distributions of provisions and the superabundance of shows, yielded very little in return. Rome, which made the provinces send her everything, never reimbursed them except with the money from the taxes, that is to say, with the very sums with which these provinces had provided her. Her so-called commerce was thus only indirect robbery. The capital, being an unproductive city, was truly an "octopus."

Speaking generally, the towns were very sparsely populated. Even in the time of the Empire's greatest prosperity, the largest towns in Gaul, Nimes, Toulouse, Autun and Treves, can never have numbered more than 50,000 inhabitants. . . . Famous towns like Marseilles, Milan, Verona, Aquileia and Naples had at all times been small. Still more was this the case when, in consequence of the disasters of the third century and of the resulting depopulation, the towns had to contract, occupying now only a quarter, a tenth or sometimes even a twentieth part of their former area. . . .

Not only was the population not dense, but its buying capacity was poor. The men of Antiquity, if they did not live in opulence, had few needs. Their food was simple and frugal, as is still that of the men of the South [Mediterranean] in our days. The lower classes lived on wheaten bread and paste (the other cereals being despised) and on vegetables. The use of meat was not common, except pork and kid, whence our word "butcher," which means one who sell's kid's flesh. Butter was a barbarian article of food and oil was preferred to it. Wine was drunk but little; even the army which was so carefully looked after, had it only every other day. Under these conditions, the trades in food-stuffs could not be thriving.

It was the same with clothing. Clothes were simple and rarely renewed. There was no real linen. Thus there was no development in the clothing industry. It did not succeed in going beyond the stage of production in private workshops, until the extension of the wool trade and the drapery industry . . . this means that these changes took place only at advanced stage of the history of the Middle Ages. Living, heating, and lighting arrangements thus remained stationary.

The population of the large towns was crowded into rented houses divided into mutually independent stories *(insulae)*. They were gloomy dwellings with insufficient or no heating, even in winter, except by means of *braseros*. For lighting a primitive oil lamp was used, a mere wick floating in oil. The furniture was very perfunctory, consisting of a bed (a tressel with cushions thrown on it), chests, tables and chairs. The citizen lived as little as possible inside his gloomy dwelling; when his work was over, if he worked, he walked in the streets, under the porticos, in the forum, or frequented the circuses, the theatre and the baths where he was forced to bathe frequently, owing to the lack of linen. Speaking generally, the psychology of the man of Antiquity differed appreciably from ours. He had few wants and his tastes were very stable. Fashion scarcely existed, and it exercised its influence only on the upper classes and not on the whole of society, as it does in our day. Moreover it changed very slowly. Dress, dwelling houses, furniture, objects of art, all tended to become stereotyped into almost unchangeable forms. Whence the monotonous and boring character of Roman civilization.

It is true that in the Roman world were to be found dazzling and colossal fortunes—in comparison with the Middle Ages or the dawn of modern times. But in the ordinary routine of their life, the rich, even in the town, lived on the products of their country estates and bought almost nothing. An exception must be made for articles of luxury which were imported from the four corners of the globe. But modern economics have taught us that the commerce in luxuries, which concerns only a small number of rich men, is absolutely inadequate to produce, stimulate and maintain a thriving industry: There was little or no middle class. Between extreme luxury and resigned or snarling poverty, there was nothing. At Rome, the richest and most splendid of all the towns, over against the 1,800 *domus* (palaces) there were 46,600 apartments swarming with a starving population. People of good birth, without any means, lived on *sportulae*. Rome was a town of beggars and remained so almost up to contemporary times.

Further, there was a profound difference between ancient and modern urban life. The modern town lives above all on industry and commerce, wherein lies its peculiar function.

It was not necessarily the same with the ancient town, above all when it was the capital of the State. People of good birth there lived on the produce of their land. Industry and commerce might thrive in addition, but they did not constitute the primary function of the town. The latter did not radiate over the neighbouring territory to fertilize, enrich and civilize it, but sucked in its means of subsistence; it was "tentacular," to use a contemporary expression.

Hence, the towns were not centres of industry connected with each other through interest or even competition. Thus there was no real industrial bourgeoisie in Antiquity, because, strictly speaking, there was no large or middle-scale industry. We will not call by the name of "large-scale industry" the enterprises started under the control of the State, for the provisioning of the capitals and the army.

Commerce

Though commerce was regarded more favourably than industry, it never reached any very great volume. Producing little, the Roman world carried little and sold little. Hence, in the absence of industry in the Roman world, commerce could not convey the products of a foreign industry. Commerce on a large scale could only concern itself with objects of luxury, the high price of which makes it possible to recover the expenses of transport. But about luxury trade we may repeat the observations concerning luxury industry. It is at bottom unproductive. Lastly, in this traffic, the balance was unfavorable for Rome and the West, which paid in money and sold nothing or practically nothing by way of merchandise. Gold and silver were thus drained towards the East and Far East.

The deep underlying cause of this languid life of business is to be sought in the psychology of the Romans. Unlike the Greeks of the Athenian and of the Hellenistic period, they were not deeply or for a long time interested in trade; they showed "little commercial jealousy" and in spite of what has been asserted, Rome never had a commercial policy.

The upper classes of society (the senatorial and equestrian classes) were turned away from commerce by prejudice and even by law. These classes, which were yet so grasping, did not possess the capitalist spirit of enterprise. Large business did not get from them the help of capital which they alone possessed and the class of real business men, with experience and enterprise, useful and respected, without which there is no real capitalist system, was not formed. . . .

Agriculture

In default of industry and commerce, could not capital be employed in agriculture? Whether capital is applied to industry or agriculture, it has been said, is a secondary consideration.

The historians who entertain these opinions have especially in view the *latifundia* [large estates] worked by means of slaves on what are maintained to be capitalist lines.

It is certain that at the end of the Republic and under the Empire, sustained efforts were made to apply to agriculture the plentiful capital which was at the disposal of the upper classes. For a man of low birth, who had made his wealth by commerce, the only means of making people forget this stain was to buy land. Small business was "sordid"; but the merchant who retired and employed his fortune in agriculture was worthy of praise.

Custom, legislation, Imperial favour, and fashion even, encouraged men to invest money in the purchase and working of large landed estates.

But the results were not proportionate to these efforts. The capitalist exploitation of the soil ended in complete failure.

The reason is that exploitation by means of slaves not only ties up large capital sums, but requires at least two other conditions in order to be remunerative, a rich soil and densely populated areas in the neighbourhood. But the most fertile parts of Italy, Gaul, etc., remained for a long time fallow; in the absence of scientific knowledge, which is of very recent growth, and also in the absence of large cattle, the greater part of the soil was soon exhausted, especially under the system of biennial rotation. The towns were very poor markets. The majority were, as we have seen, small, sparsely populated, and what was worse, far from each other, conditions which militated against their being profitable markets. There remained Rome; but being provisioned by Africa, Sicily, etc., the capital was economically like a foreign city in relation to Italy.

Let us remember that the consuming power of the population of the towns was very limited, neither meat nor wine being in demand. The transport of wine, oil, etc. (by means of earthenware vases or wine-skins) was moreover inconvenient, and that of fruits more difficult still.

Hence the large slave-worked estates knew only extensive exploitation, chiefly pasturing. They produced not so much for the market as for the upkeep of the owner, his family and clients. The *latifundia* come under domestic economy. They herald and prepare the way for feudal economy, it may be, but not at all for the capitalist system.

Thus, wherever this was possible, the landowner came to divide his estates into plots assigned to [workers called] *coloni*.

Were these *coloni* farmers in the modern sense, that is to say small capitalist owners of cattle, agricultural implements and movable stock? Certainly not. The free *colonus* had only his hands and his family to help him, but no capital; and this no doubt explains the ease with which he became bound to the soil under the Latin Empire. . . .

Thus, capitalism, when applied to agriculture, was unable to change its character of natural economy and nothing is less like capitalist economy than the agriculture of the Roman Empire. . . .

Investment and Usury

Of the landed investments we have already spoken. They were scarcely, if at all, productive. Their aim was social and snobbish and they were of small economic value. First and foremost usury flourished. . . . Usury on a large scale was approved of and it was not considered shameful to engage in it. And what usury! Knights and Senators lent money to Kings in the East then to towns, corporations and private individuals, at incredible rates of interest. The rule was 4 per cent per month; some lent only at 75 per cent or 100 per cent; Atticus, for example, who was looked upon by his contemporaries as the

King of the Knights. As he was a patron of men of letters, he has, in spite of this, left behind him the reputation of a gentleman. Brutus lent at 48 per cent. "All the great names in Roman history are connected with transactions of usury." So much for the provinces.

In Italy, even in settled times the rate of 12 per cent was legal. "Rome's great industry was usury." Money went neither to the land, nor to commerce, nor to industry. The capital of the Roman world did not feed enterprise. Being applied to usury, capital even dried up the spirit of enterprise, and by attacking the sources of wealth, it discouraged production.

This usurious, idle, and by no means capitalistic aristocracy was in addition horribly spendthrift. The luxury of the higher classes may have been exaggerated; but it remains nevertheless certain that at the end of the Roman Republic and the beginning of the Empire, senseless acts of prodigality, involving a wholesale destruction of wealth, were indulged in.

Finally, it should be observed that the Ancients had no sound conception of the nature of productive capital. . . . Roman "capitalism" had been but a thin layer swept away by the breath of the storm, and the underlying rock of natural economy very quickly came to the surface.

This return to natural economy, after the arrest of monetary economy, already marks the economic Middle Ages. Politically and socially, it is the introduction to the Middle Ages.

General Decline

With the material prosperity and stage of civilization reached by Ancient Society was bound up the stability of the Imperial regime. The economic system being in process of marked retrogression, the expenses ought to have been reduced. But to this men could not resign themselves. The Roman State, from the end of the third century, was like a ruined landlord who wants to keep up the same establishment as in the days of his prosperity. These attempts were all in vain. The State saw only one way of salvation; to bind every man by force to his occupation, to chain him and his descendants to the same post, and it established a real caste system. The reforms of Diocletian, Constantine and their successors betray the desperate struggle of an organism refusing to die, with natural economic forces which will not allow society to maintain with very reduced means a large and complex State.

E. SOURCES FOR PART I

1. Morris Jastrow, *The Civilization of Babylonia and Assyria,* Philadelphia: J.B. Lippincott & Co., 1915.
2. *Old Testament,* Genesis 1-3.
3. H.G. Evelyn-White (trans.), *Hesiod, Homeric Hymns, and Homerica,* Cambridge: Harvard Univ. Press, 1914.
4. *Thoughts of Marcus Aurelius Antonius,* trans. by John Jackson, London: Oxford Univ. Press, 1906.
5. C.H.W. Johns (ed.), *Babylonian and Assyrian Laws, Contracts, and Letters,* New York: Scriber & Sons, 1904.
6. *Old Testament,* Exodus 20-22.
7. *Plutarch Lives* in Oliver Thatcher (ed.) *The Ideas That Have Influenced Civilization,* Milwaukee: Roberts-Manchester, 1901
8. Thucydides, "Funeral Oration of Pericles," in George W. Bodsford (ed.), *A Source-Book of Ancient History,* New York: 1912.
9. Polybius, *The Histories,* trans. by Evelyn S. Shuckburgh, London: 1889.
10. *History of Herodotus,* trans. by George Rawlinson, 4th ed.; London: John Murray, 1880.
11. Juvenal's "Third Satire," in *The British*

Poets, Including Translations, trans. by John Dryden, Chiswick: 1822. vol. xlvi.
12. Petronius Arbiter, *Trimalchio's Dinner,* trans. by Harry T. Peck, New York: 1898.
13. *Works of Xenophon,* trans. by H.G. Dakyns, London: 1892.
14. Ferdinand Lot, *The End of the Ancient World and the Beginnings of the Middle Ages,* New York: Alfred A. Knopf Inc. 1931. Reprinted by permission of publisher.

II
MEDIEVAL CIVILIZATION

A. ETHICS

1. Sermon on the Mount

The words of Jesus as presented in the Gospel according to St. Matthew contain the best known and most widely quoted passages from the New Testament. In this selection we find many of the basic ethical teachings of Christianity. The reader may wish to reach his own conclusions on the essential elements of Christianity and on the practicality of these teachings in our modern "affluent society."

And seeing the multitudes, he went up into a mountain: And when he was set, his disciples came unto him: And he opened his mouth, and taught them, saying, "Blessed are the poor in spirit: for theirs is the kingdom of heaven. Blessed are they that mourn: for they shall be comforted. Blessed are the meek: for they shall inherit the earth. Blessed are they which do hunger and thirst after righteousness: for they shall be filled. Blessed are the merciful: for they shall obtain mercy. Blessed are the pure in heart: for they shall see God. Blessed are the peacemakers: for they shall be called the children of God. Blessed are they which are persecuted for righteousness' sake: for theirs is the kingdom of heaven. Blessed are ye, when men shall revile you, and persecute you, and shall say all manner of evil against you falsely, for my sake. Rejoice, and be exceeding glad: for great is your reward in heaven: for so persecuted they the prophets which were before you.

"Ye are the salt of the earth: but if the salt have lost his savour, wherewith shall it be salted? It is thenceforth good for nothing, but to be cast out, and to be trodden under foot of men. Ye are the light of the world. A city that is set on an hill cannot be hid. Neither do men light a candle, and put it under a bushel, but on a candlestick; and it giveth light unto all that are in the house. Let your light so shine before men, that they may see your good works, and glorify your Father which is in heaven.

"Think not that I am come to destroy the law, or the prophets: I am not come to destroy, but to fulfil. For verily I say unto you, till heaven and earth pass, one jot or one tittle shall in no wise pass from the law, till all be fulfilled. Whosoever therefore shall break one of these least commandments, and shall teach men so, he shall be called the least in the kingdom of heaven: but whosoever shall do and teach them, the same shall be called great in the kingdom of heaven. For I say unto you, that except your righteousness shall exceed the righteousness of the scribes and Pharisees, you shall in no case enter into the kingdom of heaven.

"Ye have heard that it was said by them of old time, Thou shalt not kill; and whosoever shall kill shall be in danger of the judgment. But I say unto you, That whosoever is angry with his brother without a cause shall be in danger of the judgment: and whosoever shall say to his brother, Ra-ca, shall be in danger of the council: but whosoever shall say, Thou fool, shall be in danger of hell fire. Therefore if thou bring thy gift to the altar, and there rememberest that thy brother hath ought against thee; leave there thy gift before the altar, and go thy way; first be reconciled to thy brother, and then come and offer thy gift.

"Ye have heard that it was said by them of old time, Thou shalt not commit adultery. But I say unto you, That whosoever looketh on a woman to lust after her hath committed adultery with her already in his heart. And if thy right eye offend thee, pluck it out, and cast it from thee: for it is profitable for thee that one of thy members should perish, and not that thy whole body should be cast into hell. And if thy right hand offend thee, cut it off, and cast it from thee: for it is profitable for thee that one of thy members should perish, and not that thy whole body should be cast into hell. It hath been said, Whosoever shall put away his wife, let him give her a writing of divorcement. But I say unto you, That whosoever shall put away his wife, saving for the cause of fornication, causeth her to commit adultery: and whosoever shall marry her that is divorced committeth adultery.

"Ye have heard that it hath been said, An eye for an eye, and a tooth for a tooth. But I say unto you. That ye resist not evil: but whosoever shall smite thee on thy right cheek, turn to him the other also. And if any man will sue thee at the law, and take away thy coat, let him have thy cloke also. And whosoever shall compel thee to go a mile, go with him twain. Give to him that asketh thee, and from him that would borrow of thee turn not thou away.

"Ye have heard that it hath been said, Thou shalt love thy neighbour, and hate thine enemy. But I say unto you, Love your enemies, bless them that curse you, do good to them that hate you, and pray for them which despitefully use you, and persecute you. After this manner therefore pray ye: Our Father which art in heaven, hallowed be thy name. Thy kingdom come. Thy will be done in earth, as it is in heaven. Give us this day our daily bread. And forgive us our debts, as we forgive our debtors. And lead us not into temptation, but deliver us from evil: For thine is the kingdom, and the power, and the glory, forever. A-men.

"For if ye forgive men their trespasses, your heavenly Father will also forgive you: But if ye forgive not men their trespasses, neither will your father forgive your trespasses.

"Lay not up for yourselves treasures upon earth, where moth and rust doth corrupt, and where thieves break through and steal. But I lay up for yourselves treasures in heaven, where neither moth nor rust doth corrupt, and where thieves do not break through nor steal: For where your treasure is, there will your heart be also. The light of the body is the eye: if therefore thine eye be single thy whole body shall be full of light. But if thine eye be evil, thy whole body shall be full of darkness. If therefore the light that is in thee be darkness, how great is that darkness!

"No man can serve two masters: for either

he will hate the one, and love the other; or else he will hold to the one, and despise the other. Ye cannot serve God and mammon. Therefore I say unto you, Take no thought for your life, what ye shall eat, or what ye shall drink; nor yet for your body, what ye shall put on. Is not the life more than meat, and the body than raiment? Behold the fowls of the air: for they sow not, neither do they reap, nor gather into barns; yet your heavenly Father feedeth them. Are ye not much better than they? Which of you by taking thought can add one cubit unto his stature? And why take ye thought for raiment? Consider the lilies of the field, how they grow; they toil not, neither do they spin: And yet I say unto you, That even Solomon in all his glory was not arrayed like one of these. Wherefore, if God so clothe the grass of the field, which to day is, and tomorrow is cast into the oven, shall he not much more clothe you, O ye of little faith? Therefore take no thought, saying, What shall we eat? or, What shall we drink? or, Wherewithal shall we be clothed? (For after all these things do the Gentiles seek.) for your heavenly Father knoweth that ye have need of all these things. But seek ye first the kingdom of God, and his righteousness; and all these things shall be added unto you. Take therefore no thought for the morrow: for the morrow shall take thought for the things of itself. Sufficient unto the day is the evil thereof.

"Judge not, that ye be not judged. For with what judgment ye judge, ye shall be judged: and with what measure ye mete, it shall be measured to you again. And why beholdest thou the mote that is in thy brother's eye, but considerest not the beam that is in thine own eye? Or how wilt thou say to thy brother, Let me pull out the mote out of thine eye; and, behold a beam is in thine own eye? Thou hypocrite, first cast out the beam out of thine own eye; and then shalt thou see clearly to cast out the mote out of thy brother's eye.

"Give not that which is holy unto the dogs, neither cast ye your pearls before swine, lest they trample them under their feet, and turn again and rend you.

"Ask, and it shall be given you; seek and ye shall find; knock, and it shall be opened unto you: For every one that asketh receiveth; and he that seeketh; and to him that knocketh it shall be opened.

"Beware of false prophets, which come to you in sheep's clothing, but inwardly they are ravening wolves. Ye shall know them by their fruits. Do men gather grapes of thorns, or figs of thistles? Even so every good tree bringeth forth good fruit; but a corrupt tree bringeth forth evil fruit. A good tree cannot bring forth evil fruit, neither can a corrupt tree bring forth good fruit. Every tree that bringeth not forth good fruit is hewn down, and cast into the fire. Wherefore by their fruits ye shall know them.

"Not every one that saith unto me, Lord, Lord, shall enter into the kingdom of heaven; but he that doeth the will of my Father which is in heaven.

"Therefore whosoever heareth these sayings of mine, and doeth them I will liken him unto a wise man, which built his house upon a rock: And it came to pass, when Jesus had ended these sayings, the people were astonished at his doctrine: For he taught them as one having authority, and not as the scribes."

2. Revelations of Mohammed

The Arabic leader Mohammed (570-632 A.D.) was the founder of Islam, one of the world's great universal religions. The following selection is taken from the Koran. The Koran is regarded by the followers of Mohammed as the final revealed word of God (Allah) completing a series of revelations going from Abraham to Jesus. Thus the sacred book of Islam indicates a relationship to the Judeo-Christian tradition.

The Second Surah

Intitled, The Cow; Revealed Partly at Mecca, and Partly at Medina

There is no doubt in this book; it is a direction of the pious, who believe in the mysteries of faith, who observe the appointed times of prayer, and distribute alms out of what we [Allah] have bestowed on them, and who believe in that revelation, which hath been sent down unto thee, and that which hath been sent down unto the prophets before thee, and have firm assurance of the life to come: these are directed by their Lord, and they shall prosper. As for the unbelievers, it will be equal to them whether thou admonish them, or do not admonish them; they will not believe. God hath sealed up their hearts and their hearing; a dimness covereth their sight, and they shall suffer a grievous punishment. . . .

O true believers, eat of the good things which we have bestowed on you for food, and return thanks unto God, if ye serve him. Verily he hath forbidden you to eat that which dieth of itself, and blood and swine's flesh, and that on which any other name but God's hath been invoked. But he who is forced by necessity, not lusting, nor returning to transgress, it shall be no crime in him if he eat of those things, for God is gracious and merciful . . . It is not righteousness that ye turn your faces in prayer towards the east and the west, but righteousness is of him who believeth in God and the last day, and the angels, and the scriptures, and the prophets; who giveth money for God's sake unto his kindred, and unto orphans, and the needy, and the stranger, and those who ask, and for redemption of captives; who is constant at prayer, and giveth alms; and of those who perform their covenant, when they have covenanted, and who behave themselves patiently in adversity, and hardships, and in time of violence; these are they who are true, and these are they who fear God. . . .

O true believers, a fast is ordained you, as it was ordained unto those before you, that ye may fear God. A certain number of days shall ye fast: but among you who shall be sick, or on a journey, shall fast an equal number of other days. And those who can keep it, and do not, must redeem their neglect by maintaining of a poor man. And he who voluntarily dealeth better with the poor man than he is obliged, this shall be better for him. But if ye fast it will be better for you, if ye knew it. The month of Ramadan shall ye fast, in which the Koran was sent down from heaven a direction unto men, and declarations of direction, and the distinction between good and evil. . . .

Perform the pilgrimage to Mecca, and the visitation of God. . . . Make provision for your journey; but the best provision is piety: and fear me, O ye of understanding. It shall be no crime in you, if ye seek an increase from your Lord, by trading during the pilgrimage. . . .

Deal not unjustly with others, and ye shall not be dealt with unjustly. If there be any debtor under a difficulty of paying his debt, let his creditor wait till it be easy for him to do it; but if ye remit it as alms, it will be better for you, if ye knew it. . . .

Whatever is in heaven and on earth is God's: and whether ye manifest that which is in your minds, or conceal it, God will call you to account for it, and will forgive whom he pleaseth, and will punish whom he pleaseth, for God is almight. . . .

The Hundred and Twelfth Surah

Intitled, The Declaration of God's Unity; Where it was Revealed is Disputed

In the Name of the Most Merciful God
Say, God is one God; the eternal God: he begetteth not, neither is he begotten: and there is not any one like unto him.

3. Medieval Mysticism, St. Francis of Assisi

St. Francis (1182-1226 A.D.) the son of an Italian cloth merchant was the most loved and admired religious personality of the Middle Ages. He has been regarded by many as the truest Christian since Christ himself. His life and teachings reflect the asceticism and other worldly outlook of the age of faith.

And from that time forth St. Francis began to taste and feel more bounteously the sweetness of divine contemplation and of divine visitations. Among which, he had one, immediate and preparatory to the imprinting of the divine stigmas, in this form. The day that goeth before the feast of the Most Holy Cross in the month of September, as St. Francis was praying in secret in his cell, the angel of God appeared to him and spoke thus to him in God's name, "I am come to comfort and adminish thee that thou humbly prepare thee and make thee ready, with all patience, to receive that which God willeth to give thee and to work in thee." St. Francis answered, "I am ready to endure patiently all things that my Lord would do with me." St. Francis began to contemplate most devoutly the Passion of Christ and His infinite love; and the fervour of devotion waxed so within him that through love and through compassion he was wholly changed into Jesus. And being thus inflamed by this contemplation, he beheld, that same morning, a seraph with six resplendent and flaming wings come down from heaven; which seraph, with swift flight, drew nigh to St. Francis so that he could discern him, and he knew clearly that he had the form of a man crucified.

Thereafter, he marvelled greatly at so stupendous and unwonted a vision, well knowing that the infirmity of the Passion doth not accord with the immortality of the seraphic spirit. And being in this wonderment, it was revealed by the seraph who appeared to him, that that vision had been shown to him in such form by divine providence, in order that he might understand he was to be changed into the express similitude of the crucified Christ in this wonderous vision, not by bodily martyrdom but by spiritual fire. Then the whole mount of La Verna seemed to flame forth with dazzling splendour, that shone and illumined all the mountains and the valleys round about, as were the sun shining on the earth. Wherefore when the shepherds that were watching in that country saw the mountain aflame and so much brightness round about they were sore afraid, according as they afterwards told the frairs, and affirmed that that flame had endured over the mount of La Verna for the space of an hour and more. Likewise, certain muleteers that were going to Romagna, arose up at the brightness of this light which shone through the windows of the inns of that country, and thinking the sun had risen, saddled and loaded their beasts. And as they went their way, they saw the said light wane and the real sun rise. Now Christ appeared in that same seraphic vision, and revealed to St. Francis certain secret and high things that St. Francis would never, during his life, disclose to any man; but, after his death, he revealed them, according as is set forth hereafter. And the words were these, "Knowest thou," said Christ, "what I have done to thee? I have given thee the stigmas that are the marks of my Passion, in order that thou be My standard-bearer. And even as I, on the day of my death, descended into limbo and delivered all the souls I found there by virtue of these My stigmas, so do I grant to thee that every year, on the day of thy death, thou mayst go to purgatory and deliver all the souls thou shalt find there of thy three orders—Minors, Sisters, and Penitents—and others likewise that shall have had great devotion to thee, and thou shalt lead them up to the glory of paradise in order that thou be conformed to Me in thy death, even as thou art in thy life." This wondrous vision vanished, after a great space, this secret converse left in the heart of St. Francis a burning flame of divine love, exceeding great, and in his flesh, a marvellous image and imprint of the Passion of Christ.

4. On the Existence of God, St. Thomas Aquinas

St. Thomas Aquinas (1225-1274) an Italian Dominican and professor of theology at the University of Paris, is considered the greatest scholastic philosopher of the middle ages. His **Summary of Theology** *excerpted below is his most influential work and is regarded as a systematic encyclopedia of medieval learning.*

First Article
Whether the Existence of God is Self-Evident?

We proceed thus to the First Article:—

Objection 1. It seems that the Existence of God is self-evident. Those things are said to be self-evident to us the knowledge of which is naturally implanted in us, as we can see in regard to first principles. But the Damascene says that, *the knowledge of God is naturally implanted in all* Therefore the Existence of God is self-evident.

Objection 2. Further, those things are said to be self-evident which are known as soon as the terms are known, which the Philosopher says is true of the first principles of demonstration. Therefore, because as soon as the word 'God' is understood it exists mentally, it also follows that it exists actually. Therefore the proposition that God exists is self-evident.

Objection 3. Further, the existence of Truth is self-evident; for whoever denies the existence of Truth concedes that Truth does not exist. Now, if Truth does not exist, then the proposition 'Truth does not exist' is true. But if there is anything true, there must be Truth. God is Truth itself: *I am the way, the truth, and the life.* Therefore the proposition that God exists is self-evident.

On the contrary, No one can mentally admit the opposition of what is self-evident; as is clear from the Philosopher, concerning the first principles of demonstration. The opposition of the proposition 'God' can be mentally admitted: *The fool hath said in his heart, There is no God.* Therefore, that God exists is not self-evident.

I answer that, A thing can be self-evident in either of two ways; on the one hand, self-evident in itself, though not to us; on the other, self-evident in itself, and to us. A proposition is self-evident because the predicate is included in the notion of the subject, as 'Man is an animal,' for animal is contained in the formal idea of man. Therefore I say that this proposition, 'God exists,' of itself is self-evident, for the predicate is the same as the subject; because God is His Own Existence. For as much as we do not know the Essence of God, the proposition is not self-evident to us; but needs to be proved by such things as are more evident to us, though less evident in their nature—namely, by effects.

Reply Objection 1. To know that God exists in a general and indefinite way is implanted in us by nature, inasmuch as God is man's beatitude. For man naturally desires happiness, and what is naturally desired by a man must be naturally known to him. This, however, is not to know absolutely that God exists; as to know that Peter is approaching, even though it is Peter who is approaching.

Reply Objection 2. Perhaps not everyone who hears this word 'God' may understand it to signify something than which nothing better can be imagined, seeing that some have believed God to be a body. Yet, granted that everyone understands that by this word 'God' is signified something than which nothing greater can be imagined, nevertheless, it does not therefore follow that he understands that what the word signifies exists actually, but only that it exists mentally. Nor can it be argued logically that it actually exists, unless it be admitted that there exists something than which nothing greater can be imagined; and this precisely is not admitted by those who hold that God does not exist.

Reply Objection 3. The existence of truth in a general way is self-evident, but the existence of a Primal Truth is not self-evident to us.

Third Article
Whether God Exists?

We proceed thus to the Third Article:—

Objection 1. It seems that God does not exist; because if one of two contraries be infinite, the other would be altogether destroyed. But the word 'God' means that He is infinite goodness. If, therefore, God existed, there would be no evil discoverable; but there is evil in the world. Therefore God does not exist.

Objection 2. Further, it is superfluous to suppose that what can be accounted for by a few principles has been produced by many. But it seems that everything that appears in the world can be accounted for by other principles, supposing God did not exist. For all natural things can be reduced to one principle, which is nature; and all things that happen intentionally can be reduced to one principle, which is human reason, or will. Therefore there is no need to suppose God's existence.

On the contrary, It is said in the person of God: *I am Who am* (Exod. iii. 14).

I answer that, The existence of God can be proved in five ways.

The first and more manifest way is the argument from motion. It is certain and evident to our senses that some things are in motion. Whatever is in motion is moved by another, for nothing can be in motion except it have a potentiality for that towards which it is being moved; whereas a thing moves inasmuch as it is in act. Therefore, whatever is in motion must be put in motion by another. Therefore it is necessary to arrive at a First Mover, put in motion by no other; and this everyone understands to be God.

The second way is from the formality of efficient causation. In the world of sense we find there is an order of efficient causation. Therefore it is necessary to put forward a First Efficient Cause, to which everyone gives the name of God.

The third was is taken from possibility and necessity, and runs thus. We find in nature things that could either exist or not exist, since they are found to be generated, and to corrupt; and, consequently, they can exist, and then not exist. It is impossible for these always to exist, for that which can one day cease to exist must at some time have not existed. It is impossible to go on to infinity in necessary things which have their necessity caused by another, as has been already proved in regard to efficient causes. Therefore we cannot but postulate of some being having of itself its own necessity, and not receiving it from another, but rather causing in others their necessity. This all men speak of as God.

The fourth way is taken from the gradation to be found in things. Among beings there are some more and some less good, true, noble, and the like. Therefore there must also be something which is to all beings the cause of their being, goodness, and every other perfection; and this we call God.

The fifth way is taken from the governance of the world; for we see that things which lack intelligence, such as natural bodies, act for some purpose. Therefore some intelligent being exists by whom all natural things are ordained towards a definite purpose; and this being we call God.

Reply Objection 1. As Augustine says: *Since God is wholly good. He would not allow any evil to exist in His works, unless His omnipotence and goodness were such as to bring good even out of evil.* This is part of the infinite goodness of God, that He should allow evil to exist, and out of it produce good.

Reply Objection 2. Since nature works for a determinate and under the direction of a higher agent, whatever is done by nature must needs be traced back to God, as to its first cause. So also whatever is done designedly must also be traced back to some higher cause other than human reason or will, for these can suffer change and are defective; whereas things capable of motion and of defect must be traced back to an immovable and self-necessary first principle.

B. LAW

5. Salic Law

Once the German tribes settled into Western Europe they wrote down their laws. The most famous of these is that of the Salian Franks. It is the section on the rights of women to inherit which would disrupt future events in Europe.

Title I. Concerning Summonses: 1. If any one be summoned before the "Thing" [an assembly of elders and interested parties] by the King's law, and do not come, he shall be sentenced to 15 shillings.

2. But he who summons another, and does not come himself, shall, if a lawful impediment have not delayed him, be sentenced to 15 shillings, to be paid him whom he summoned.

3. And he who summons another shall walk with witness to the home of that man, and, if he be not at home, shall bid the wife or any one of the family to make known to him that he has been summoned to court.

Title XI. Concerning Thefts or House-

breakings of Freemen: 1. If any freeman steal, outside of the house, something worth 2 denars, he shall be sentenced to 35 shillings.

Title XII. Concerning Thefts or Housebreakings on the Part of Slaves 1. If a slave steal, outside of the house, something, he shall, besides paying the worth of the object and the fines for delay, be stretched out and receive 120 blows.

2. But if he steal something worth 40 denars, he shall either be castrated or pay 6 shillings. But the lord of the slave who committed the theft shall restore to the plaintiff the worth of the object and fines for delay.

Title XIII. Concerning Rape Committed by Freemen 1. If three men carry off a free born girl, they shall be compelled to pay 30 shillings.

4. But those who commit rape shall be compelled to pay 63 shillings.

8. But if a free woman have followed a slave of her own will, she shall lose her freedom.

9. If a freeborn man shall have taken an alien bondswoman, he shall suffer similarly.

10. If anybody take an alien spouse and join her to himself in matrimony, he shall be sentenced to 63 shillings.

Title XIV. Concerning Assault and Robbery: 1. If any one have assaulted and plundered a free man, and it be proved on him, he shall be sentenced to 63 shillings.

2. If a Roman have plundered a Salian Frank, the above law shall be observed.

3. But if a Frank have plundered a Roman, he shall be sentenced to 35 shillings.

Title XXX. Concerning Insults: 3. If any one, man or woman, shall have called a woman harlot, and shall have not been able to prove it, he shall be sentenced to 45 shillings.

Title LIX. Concerning Private Property: 1. If any man die and leave no sons, if the father and mother survive, they shall inherit.

2. If the father and mother do not survive, and he leave brothers and sisters, they shall inherit.

3. But if there are none, the sisters of the father shall inherit.

4. But if there are no sisters of the father, the sisters of the mother shall claim that inheritance.

5. If there are none of these, the nearest relatives on the father's side shall succeed to that inheritance.

6. But of Salic land no portion of the inheritance shall come to a woman: but the whole inheritance of the land shall come to the male sex.

6. Justinian's Institutes

Although the Western Roman Empire was destroyed, it continued in the East for another thousand years. It was under the rule of Emperor Justinian (527-65) that the earlier Roman Laws were codified and eventually were passed back to the West.

The Emperor Caesar Flavius Justinianus, Vanquisher of the Alamani, Goths, Franks, Germans . . . Triumphant Conqueror, Ever August, to the Youth Desirous of Studying the Law. Greetings

The Imperial majesty should be not only made glorious by arms, but also strengthened by laws, that, alike in time of peace and in time of war, the state may be well governed, and that the emperor may not only be victorious in the field of battle, but also may by every legal means repel the iniquities of men who abuse the laws, and may at once religiously uphold justice and triumph over his conquered enemies.

1. By our incessant labours and great care, with the blessing of God, we have attained this double end. The barbarian nations reduced under our yoke know our efforts in war; to which also Africa and very many other provinces bear witness, which, after so long an interval, have been restored to the dominion of Rome and our empire, by our victories gained through the favour of heaven. All nations moreover are governed by laws which we have either promulgated or arranged.

2. When we had arranged and brought into perfect harmony the hitherto confused mass of imperial constitutions, we then extended our care to the endless volumes of ancient law; and, have now completed, through the favour of heaven, a work we once despaired of.

3. We summoned the most eminent Tribonian, master and ex-quaestor of our palace, together with the illustrious Theophilus and Dorotheus, professors of law, all of whom have on many occasions proved to us their ability, legal knowledge and obedience to our orders; and we specially charge them to compose, under our authority and advice, Institutes, so that you may no more learn the first elements of law from old and erroneous sources, but apprehend them by the clear light of imperial wisdom; and that your minds and ears may receive nothing that is useless or misplaced, but only what obtains in actual practice. So that whereas, formerly, the foremost among you could scarcely, after four years' study, read the imperial constitutions, you may now commence your studies by reading them, you who have been thought worthy of an honour and a happiness so great as that the first and last lessons in the knowledge of the law should issue for you from the mouth of the emperor.

4. When therefore, by the assistance of the same eminent person Tribonian and that of other illustrious and learned men, we had compiled the fifty books, called Digests or Pandects, in which is collected the whole ancient law, we directed that these Institutes should be divided into four books, which might serve as the first elements in the whole science of law.

5. In these books a brief exposition is given of the ancient laws, and of those also, which overshadowed by disuse, have been again brought to light by our imperial authority.

6. These four books of Institutes thus compiled, from all the Institutes left us by the ancients, and chiefly from the commentaries of our Gaius, both from his Institutes, and his Journal, and also from many other commentaries, were presented to us by the three learned men we have above named. We read and examined them, and have accorded to them all the force of our constitutions.

7. Receive, therefore, with eagerness, and study with cheerful diligence, these our laws, and show yourselves being able, when your course of legal study is completed, to govern our empire in the different portions that may be entrusted to your care.

Given at Constantinople on the eleventh day of the calends of December, in the third consulate of the Emperor Justinian, ever August.

7. Administrative Directives of Charlemagne

For a third of a millennium Western Europe was politically in decline—the so-called Dark Ages. The one bright spot was the Carolingian rule in Frankland. It was the most outstanding king of this dynasty who helped turn Europe around. Charlemagne was a warrior, reformer, educator, and administrator, who was determined to return the West to its former greatness. Although not successful in all of his endeavors, he attempted to guarantee justice by a system of courts and written laws.

Let no one, through his cleverness or astuteness, dare to oppose or thwart the written law, as many are wont to do, or the judicial sentence passed upon him, or to do injury to the churches of God or the poor or the widows or the wards or any Christian. But all shall live entirely in accordance with God's precept, justly and under a just rule, and each one shall be admonished to live in harmony with his fellows in his business or profession; the canonical clergy ought to observe in every respect a canonical life without heeding base gain, nuns ought to keep diligent watch over their lives, laymen and the secular clergy ought rightly to observe their laws without malicious fraud, and all ought to live in mutual charity and perfect peace. And let the *missi* themselves make a diligent investigation whenever any man claims that an injustice has been done to him by any one, just as they desire to deserve the grace of omnipotent God and to keep their fidelity promised to Him, so that entirely in all cases everywhere, in accordance with the will and fear of God, they shall administer the law fully and justly in the case of the holy churches of God and of the poor, of wards and widows and of the whole people.

First, that each one voluntarily shall strive, in accordance with his knowledge and ability, to live wholly in the holy service of God in accordance with the precept of God and in accordance with his own promise, because the lord emperor is unable to give all individually the necessary care and discipline.

Secondly, that no man, either through perjury or any other wile or fraud, on account of the flattery or gift of any one, shall refuse to give back or dare to abstract or conceal a serf of the lord emperor or a district or land or anything that belongs to him; and that no one shall presume, through perjury or other wile, to conceal or abstract his fugitive fiscaline serfs who unjustly and fraudulently say that they are free.

That no one shall presume to rob or do any injury fraudulently to the churches of God or widows or orphans or pilgrims; for the lord emperor himself, after God and His saints, as constituted himself their protector and defender.

That no one shall dare to lay waste a benefice of the lord emperor, or to make it his own property.

That no one shall presume to neglect a summons to war from the lord emperor; and that no one of the counts shall be so presumptuous as to date to dismiss thence any one of those who owe military service, either on account of relationship or flattery or gifts from any one.

That no one shall presume to impede at all in any way a ban or command of the lord emperor, or to dally with his work or to impede or to lessen or in any way to act contrary to his will or commands. And that no one shall dare to neglect to pay his dues or tax.

That no one, for any reason, shall make a practice in court of defending another unjustly, either from any desire of gain when the cause is weak, or by impeding a just judgment by his skill in reasoning, or by a desire of oppressing when the cause is weak. But each one shall answer for his own cause or tax or debt unless any one is infirm or ignorant of pleading; for these the *missi* or the chiefs who are in the court or the judge who knows the case in question shall plead before the court; or if it is necessary, such a person may be allowed as is acceptable to all and knows the case well; but this shall be done wholly according to the convenience of the chiefs or *missi* who are present. But in every case it shall be done in accordance with justice and the law; and that no one shall have the power to impede justice by a gift, reward, or any kind of evil flattery or from any hindrance of relationship. And that no one shall unjustly consent to another in anything, but that with all zeal and goodwill all shall be prepared to carry out justice.

For all the above mentioned ought to be observed by the imperial oath.

8. Feudal Contracts

Medieval man lived under feudalism, which replaced the previous concept of man-to-government with a man-to-man one. Loyalty was from vassal-to-overlord. The three parts of selection eight are examples of that.

Grant of a Fief, 1200

I, Thiebault, count palatine of Troyes, make known to those present and to come that I have given in fee to Jocelyn d'Avalon and his heirs the manor which is called Gillencourt, and whatever the same Jocelyn shall be able to acquire in the same manor I have granted to him and his heirs in augmentation of that fief. I have granted, moreover, to him that in no free manor of mine will I retain men who are of this gift. The same Jocelyn, moreover, on account of this has become my liege man, having, however, his allegiance to Gerard d'Arcy, and to the lord duke of Burgundy, and to Peter count of Auxerre. Done at Chouaude, by my own witness, in the year of the Incarnation of our Lord 1200 in the month of January. Given by the hand of Walter, my chancellor; note of Milo.

Legal Rules for Military Service, 1270

The baron and all vassals of the king are bound to appear before him when he shall summon them, and to serve him at their own expense for forty days and forty nights, with as many knights as each one owes; and he is able to exact from them these services when he wishes and when he has need of them. And if the king wishes to keep them more than forty days at their own expense, they are not bound to remain if they do not wish it. And if the king wishes to keep them at his expense for the defence of the realm, they are bound to remain. And if the king wishes to lead them outside of the kingdom, they need not go unless they wish to, for they have already served their forty days and forty nights.

The Ceremony of Doing Homage and Swearing Fealty

Through the whole remaining part of the day those who had been previously enfeoffed, by the most pious Count Charles did homage to the [new] count, taking up now again their fiefs and offices and whatever they had before rightfully and legitimately obtained. On Thursday, the seventh of April, homages were again made to the count, being completed in the following order of faith and security.

First they did their homage thus. The count asked the vassal if he were willing to become completely his man, and the other replied, "I am willing;" and with hands clasped, placed between the hands of the count, they were bound together by a kiss.

Secondly, he who had done homage gave his fealty to the representative of the count in these words, "I promise on my faith that I will in future be faithful to Count William and will observe my homage to him completely against all persons, in good faith and without deceit." And, thirdly, he took his oath to this upon the relics of the saints. Afterward the count, with a little rod which he held in his hand, gave investitures to all who by this agreement had given their security and accompanying oath.

9. Peace and Truce of God

Fighting dominated feudalism and the masses suffered. As the nobility clashed, it was the land and the lives of the peasants which were torn apart. In an attempt to stop Christians from killing Christians the Church invoked the Peace and Truce of God, which restricted the time and place of conflict. And incidentally this became the origin of our concept of holidays-holydays.

1. For the salvation of your souls, we beseech all you who fear God and believe in him and have been redeemed by his blood, to follow the footsteps of God, and to keep peace one with another, that you may obtain eternal peace and quiet with Him.

2. This is the peace or truce of God which we have received from heaven through the inspiration of God, and we beseech you to accept it and observe it even as we have done; namely, that all Christians, friends and enemies, neighbors and strangers, should keep true and lasting peace one with another from vespers on Wednesday to sunrise on Monday so that during these four days and five nights, all persons may have peace, and, trusting in this peace, may go about their business without fear of their enemies.

3. All who keep the peace and truce of God shall be absolved of their sins by God, the omnipotent Father, and His Son Jesus Christ, and the Holy Spirit, and by St. Mary with the choir of virgins, and St. Michael with the choir of angels, and St. Peter with all the saints and all the faithful, now and forever.

4. Those who have promised to observe the truce and have wilfully violated it, shall be excommunicated by God the omnipotent Father, and His Son Jesus Christ, and the Holy Spirit, from the communion of all saints of God, shall be accursed and despised here and in the future world, shall be damned with . . . Judas [to the] depths of hell, as was Pharaoh in the midst of the sea, unless they make such satisfaction as is described in the following:

5. If anyone has killed another on the days of the truce of God, he shall be exiled and driven from the land and shall make a pilgrimage to Jerusalem, spending his exile there. If anyone has violated the truce of God in any other way, he shall suffer the penalty prescribed by the secular laws and shall do double the penance prescribed by the canons.

6. We believe it is just that he should suffer both secular and spiritual punishment if we break the promise which we have made to keep the peace. For we believe that this peace was given to us from heaven by God. . . .

7. We have vowed and dedicated these four days to God: Thursday, because it is the day of his ascension; Friday, because it is the day of his passion; Saturday, because it is the day in which he was in the tomb; and Sunday, because it is the day of his resurrection; on that day no labor shall be done and no one shall be in fear of his enemy.

10. Magna Carta

When King John of England attempted to usurp the privileges of the nobility, they revolted against his tyranny. When he was in their power they made him sign the "Great Charter." There was little original in it—containing guarantees from previous reigns. It was also meant primarily for the nobility, but eventually became the basis of the "Rights of Englishmen."

1. That the English Church shall be free, and shall have her whole rights and her liberties inviolable . . . .

We have also granted to all the freemen of our Kingdom, for us and our heirs, forever, all the underwritten Liberties, to be enjoyed and held by them and by their heirs, from us and from our heirs.

2. If any of our Earls or Barons, or others who hold of us in chief by military service, shall die, and at his death his heir shall be of full age, and shall owe a relief, he shall have his inheritance by the ancient relief; that is to say, the heir or heirs of an Earl, a whole Earl's Barony for one hundred pounds; the heir of a Knight, for a whole Knight's fee, by one hundred shillings at most; and he who owes less, shall give less, according to the ancient custom of fees.

7. A widow after the death of her husband shall immediately, and without difficulty, have her marriage and her inheritance; nor shall she give anything for her dower, or for her marriage, or for her inheritance, which her husband and she held at the day of his death; and she may remain in her husband's house forty days after his death, within which time her dower shall be assigned.

8. No widow shall be distrained to marry herself, while she is willing to live without a husband; but yet she shall give security that she will not marry herself without our consent, if she hold of us, or without the consent of the lord of whom she does hold, if she hold of another.

9. Neither we, nor our Bailiffs, will seize any land or rent for any debt, while the chattels of the debtor are sufficient for the payment of the debt . . . they shall have the lands and rents of the debtor, until satisfaction be made to them for the debt which they had before paid for him, unless the principal debtor can shew himself acquitted thereof against the said sureties.

10. If any one hath borrowed anything from the jews, more or less, and die before that debt be paid, the debt shall pay no interest so long as the heir shall be under age, of whomsoever he may hold; and if that debt shall fall into our hands, we will not take anything except the chattel contained in the bond.

12. No scutage nor aid shall be imposed in our kingdom, unless by the common council of our kingdom; excepting to redeem our person, to make our eldest son a knight, and once to marry our eldest daughter, and not for these, unless a reasonable aid shall be demanded.

13. . . .the City of London shall have all its ancient liberties, and its free customs, as well by land as by water. Furthermore, we will and grant that all other Cities, Burghs, and Towns, and Ports, should have all their liberties and free customs.

15. We will not give leave to any one, for the future, to take an aid of his own free men, except for redeeming his own body, and for making his eldest son a knight, and for marrying once his eldest daughter; and not that unless it be a reasonable aid.

16. None shall be distrained to do more service for a Knight's fee, nor for any other free tenement, than what is due from thence.

17. Common Pleas shall not follow our Court, but shall be held in any certain place.

28. No Constable nor other Bailiff of ours shall take the corn or other goods of any one without instantly paying money for them, unless he can obtain respite from the free-will of the seller.

29. No Constable shall compel any Knight to give money for castle-guard, if he be willing to perform it in his own person, or by another man if he cannot perform it himself for a reasonable cause; and if we have carried or sent him into the army he shall be excused from castle-guard, according to the time that he shall be in the army by our command.

30. No Sheriff nor Bailiff of ours, nor any other person shall take the horses or carts of any free-man for the purpose of carriage, without the consent of the said free-man.

31. Neither we, nor our Bailiffs, will take another man's wood . . . unless by the consent of him to whom the wood belongs.

35. There shall be one measure of wine throughout all our kingdom, and one measure of ale, and one measure of corn. . . . Also it shall be the same with weights as with measures.

38. No Bailiffs, for the future, shall put any man to his law, upon his own simple affirmation, without credible witnesses produced for that purpose.

39. No free-man shall be seized, or imprisoned, or dispossessed, or outlawed, or in any way destroyed; nor will we condemn him, nor will we commit him to prison, excepting by the legal judgment of his peers, or by the laws of the land.

41. All Merchants shall have safety and security in coming into England, and going out of England, and in staying and in traveling through England, as well by land as by water, to buy and sell, without any unjust exactions, according to ancient and right customs, excepting in the time of war, and if they be of a country at war against us: and if such are found in our land at the beginning of a war, they shall be apprehended without injury of their bodies and goods, until it be known to us, or to our Chief Justiciary, how the Merchants of our country are treated who are found in the country at war against us. . . .

45. We will not make Justiciaries, Constables, Sheriffs, or Bailiffs, excepting such as know the laws of the land, and are well disposed to observe them.

46. All Barons who have founded Abbeys, which they hold by Charters from the Kings of England, or by ancient tenure' shall have the custody of them when they become vacant, as they ought to have.

54. No man shall be apprehended or imprisoned on the appeal of a woman for the death of any other man than her husband.

60. Also all these customs and liberties aforesaid, which we have granted to be held in our Kingdom, for so much of it as belongs to us, all our subjects, as well clergy as laity, shall observe towards their tenants as far as concerns them.

C. SOCIETY

11. Description of a Serf, France—13th Century

As with most Medieval literary works, **Aucassin and Nicolet,** *a French ballad, dealt principally with the life and experiences of the nobility. However, this brief passage does provide the reader with a glimpse of the common man, a Medieval serf. Note how the serf is perceived by the noble Aucassin. What insight on social interaction during the Middle Ages do we gain from this selection?*

"All down an old road, and grassgrown, he [Aucassin] fared, when anon, looking along the way before him, he saw such an one as I shall tell you. Tall was he, and great of growth, laidly [loathsome] and marvelous to look upon; his head huge, and black as charcoal, and more than the breath of a hand between his two eyes, and great cheeks, and a big nose and broad, big nostrils and ugly, and thick lips redder than a collop [a slice of meat], and great teeth yellow and ugly, and he was shod with hosen and shoon of bull's hide, bound with cords of bark over the knee, and all about him a great cloak twofold, and he leaned on a grievous cudgel, and Auccassin came unto him, and was afraid when he beheld him."

12. Fourteenth Century Plague, Boccaccio

This selection, taken from the prologue of **The Decameron** *by Giovanni Boccaccio (1313-1375), shows the responses of Italian society to the danger of the Black Death. Notice how easily "law and order" as well as Christian ethics were abandoned by the threat of the plague. Has contemporary man reacted differently to his crises?*

When the evil [the plague] had become universal in Florance, the hearts of all the inhabitants were closed to feelings of humanity. They fled from the sick and all that belonged to them, hoping by these means to save themselves. Others shut themselves up in their houses, with their wives, their children. . . . None was allowed access to them; no intelligence of death or sickness was permitted to reach their ears; and they spent their time in singing and music and other pastimes.

Others, on the contrary, considered eating and drinking to excess, amusements of all descriptions, the indulgence of every gratification, and an indifference to what was passing around them as the best medicine, and acted accordingly. They wandered day and night from one tavern to another, and feasted without moderation or bounds. In this way they endeavored to avoid all contact with the sick, and abandoned their houses and property to chance. . . .

Amid this general lamentation and woe, the influence and authority of every law, human and divine, vanished. Most of those who were in office had been carried off by the plague, or lay sick, or had lost so many members of their families that they were unable to attend to their duties; so that thenceforth everyone acted as he thought proper. Others, in their mode of living, chose a middle course. They ate and drank what they pleased, and walked abroad, carrying odoriferous flowers, herbs, or spices, which they smelt at from time to time, in order to invigorate the brain and to avert the baneful influence of the air, infected by the sick and by the innumerable corpses of those who died of the plague. Others carried their precaution still further, and thought the surest way to escape death was by flight. They therefore left the city; women as well as men abandoning their dwellings and their relations, and retiring into the country. . . .

Thus it was that one citizen fled from another—a neighbor from his neighbors—a relation from his relations; and in the end, so completely had terror extinguished every kindlier feeling that the brother forsook his brother, the sister the sister, the wife her husband, and at last even the parent his own offspring, and abandoned them, unvisited and unsoothed, to their fate.

13. Ordinance Concerning Laborers and Servants, England—1349

The fact that an estimated 50 percent of England's population had died from the Black Death had tremendous social and economic implications. This selection from a royal decree issued by Edward III reflects that the common laborers were evidently in a position to demand improvements in their circumstances and wages. Does this 1349 Ordinance bear any resemblance to those of ancient or contemporary times?

That every man and woman of our kingdom of England of whatever condition, free or bond, ablebodied, and within the age of sixty years, not living by trade or practicing a certain craft, or having of his own by which he may live, or his own land in the tillage of which he may occupy himself, and not serving another, if, his station considered, he be needed to serve in appropriate service, he shall be bound to serve him who so requires him.

And if any such man or woman, being required to serve, will not do the same and it is proved by two true men before the sheriff, the bailiff, lord, or constable of the town where this happens, he shall immediately be taken by . . . put in the nearest jail there to remain under strict custody until he finds surety to serve in the aforesaid manner.

And if any reaper, mower, or other workman or servant of what ever status or condition, retained in any man's service, leaves the said service without reasonable cause or permission before the term agreed, he shall undergo the penalty of imprisonment.

And no man shall pay or promise to pay anyone any more wages . . . or salary then the accustomed one as aforementioned. Nor shall anyone in any other manner demand or receive the same under penalty of double that which shall be so paid, promised, demanded, or received to be given to him who thereby shall feel himself injured.

And saddlers, pelterers, whittawyers, cordwainers, tailors, smiths, carpenters, masons, tilers, shipwrights, carters, and all other artisans and laborers shall not take for their labor and workmanship more than what was accustomed to be paid to such persons in the twentieth year and other common years preceding, as aforementioned, in the places where they shall happen to work. And if anyone shall receive more, he shall be committed to the nearest jail. . . .

And butchers, fishmongers, hostelers, brewers, bakers, poulterers, and all other sellers of all sorts of victuals shall be bound to sell the victuals for a reasonable price having regard for the price that such victuals are sold in nearby places so that such sellers have moderate profit—not excessive ones but those to be reasonably required by the distance of the places whence the said victuals are carried. And if any sell such victuals in any other manner, and be convicted . . . he shall pay double what he so received to the injured party or in default of him to any other that will prosecute in this matter.

And because many sturdy beggars, as long as they can live by begging, refuse to labor and give themselves up to idleness and sin and sometimes to theft and other infamies, no one under the aforementioned penalty of imprisonment shall presume in the guise of piety or alms to give anything to such who are well able to labor or to aid them in their slothfulness, so that by this they may be compelled to labor for the necessities of life.

14. Serf Family, Creed of Piers Plowman

This reading also comes from fourteenth century England. Here we find a vivid description of the living conditions and plight of a common rural family. The reader might wish to consider the similarities and differences between the fourteenth century English serf and the thirteenth century French serf found in an earlier selection.

"And as I went my way, weeping for sorrow,
I saw a poor man o'er the plow bending.
His coat was of a clout that cary was called,
His hood was full of holes and his hair sticking out,
His shoes were patched and clouted full thick,
His toes peeped out as he the ground trod,
His hose o'erhung his gaiters on every side,
All befouled with mud, as he the plow followed.
Two mittens had he, scanty, and made all of rags,
And the fingers were worn out and filled full of mud.
This wight was bemired in the mud almost to the ankle;
Four oxen were before him, that feeble had become,
One might reckon rib, so rueful were they.
His wife walked by him with a long goad,
In a cutted skirt cutted full high,
Wrapped in a winnowing sheet to keep her from the weather;
Barefoot on the bare ice, so that the blood followed.
And at the field's end lay a little bowl
And therein lay a little child wrapped in rags,
And twain of two years old upon another side;
And all of them sang a song that sorrow was to hear.

They cried all a cry, a sorrowful note,
And the poor man sighed sore, and said, "Children, be still.' "

D. ECONOMICS

15. The Wealth of Constantinople, Robert of Clari

This one page contemporary account of Constantinople's riches would be exceedingly difficult to beat either as an account of economic largess or as an imaginative and descriptive exercise on luxury and opulence. It is no wonder that a latter day medievalist (or even a modernist) found such wealth excitingly breathtaking.

Afterwards it was ordered that all the wealth of the spoils should be brought to a certain church in the city. The wealth was brought there, and they took ten knights, high men, of the pilgrims and ten of the Venetians who were thought to be honorable, and they set them to guard this wealth. So the wealth was brought there. And it was so rich, and there were so many rich vessels of gold and silver and cloths of gold and so many rich jewels, that it was a fair marvel, the great wealth that was brought there. Not since the world was made, was there ever seen or won so great a treasure or so noble or so rich, not in the time of Alexander nor in the time of Charlemagne nor before nor after. Nor do I think, myself, that in the forty richest cities of the world there had been so much wealth as was found in Constantinople. For the Greeks say that two thirds of the wealth of this world is in Constantinople and the other third scattered throughout the world. And the very ones who were to guard the wealth took gold ornaments and whatever else they wanted and robbed the treasure. And each one of the rich men took gold ornaments or cloth of silk and gold or anything else he wanted and carried it off. So in this way they began to rob the treasure, so that nothing was shared with the common people of the host or the poor knights or the sergeants who had helped to win the treasure, save the plain silver, like the silver pitchers which the ladies of the city used to carry to the baths. And the other wealth that remained to be divided was concealed in such evil ways as I have told you. But in any event the Venetians had their half, and the precious stones and the great treasure that remained to be divided went such evil ways as I shall tell you later.

16. Guild Restrictions

This is a short but quaint and colorful depiction of "Guild Restrictions." The message is more than mood, for it is a balanced and cautionary note: while the guild system was part capitalism, it was mainly a new manifestation of medieval economic feudalism.

. . . In the first place,—that no one of the trade of spurriers shall work longer than from the beginning of the day until curfew ring out . . . by reason that no man can work so neatly by night as by day. And many persons of the said trade, who compass how to practice deception in their work, desire to work by night rather than by day; and then they introduce false iron, and iron that has been cracked, for tin, and also they put gilt on false copper, and cracked. And further,—many of the said trade are wandering about all day, without working at all at their trade; and then, when they have become drunk and frantic, they take to their work, to the annoyance of the sick, and all their neighborhood, as well by reason of the broils that arise between them and the strange folks who are dwelling among them. And then they blow up their fires so vigorously, that their forges begin all at once to blaze to the great peril of themselves and of all the neighborhood around. And then, too, all the neighbors are much in dread of the sparks, which so vigorously issue forth in all directions from the mouths of the chimneys in their forges. By reason thereof it seems unto them that working by night should be put an end to, in order such false work and such perils to avoid: and therefore the mayor and the alderman do will, by the assent of the good folks of the said trade, and for the common profit, that from henceforth such time for working, and such false work made in the trade, shall be forbidden. . . .

Also that no one of the said trade shall hang his spurs out on Sundays, or any other days that are double feasts; but only a sign indicating his business: and such spurs as they shall so sell, they are to show and sell within their shops, without exposing them without, or opening the doors or windows of their shops, on the pain aforesaid.

Also . . . that no one shall cause to be sold, or exposed for sale, any manner of old spurs for new ones, or shall garnish or change them for new ones.

Also that no one of the said trade shall take an apprentice for a less term than seven years. . . .

Also that no one of the said trade shall receive the apprentice, serving-man or journeyman of another in the same trade, during the term agreed upon between his master and him; or the pain aforesaid.

Also that no alien of another country, or foreigner of this country, shall follow or use the said trade, unless he is enfranchised before the mayor, alderman and chamberlain; and that by witness and surety of the good folks of the said trade, who will undertake for him as to his loyalty and his good behavior.

Also, that no one of the said trade shall work on Saturdays, after Noon has been rung out in the City; and not from that hour until Monday morning following.

E. SOURCES FOR PART II

1. *New Testament,* "The Gospel According to St. Matthew."
2. *The Koran,* trans, by George Sale, Philadelphia: J.B. Lippincott Co., 1888.
3. Oliver J. Thatcher and Edgar H. McNeal, *A Source Book for Medieval History,* New York: Charles Scribners & Sons, 1905.
4. St. Thomas Aquinas, *Summa Theologia,* trans. by the Fathers of the English Dominican Province, New York: Benziger Bros., 1911.
5. Ernest F. Henderson (ed.), *Select Documents of the Middle Ages,* London: George Bell & Sons, 1905.
6. *Institutes of Justinian,* trans. by Thomas C. Sanders, London: Longsman, Green, 1874.
7. University of Pennsylvania, *Translations and Reprints From Original Sources of European History,* Philadelphia: 1897-ff, Vol. VI, 5.
8. *Ibid,* IV, 3.
9. Thatcher & McNeal, *Op.Cit.*
10. Boyd C. Barrington (ed.), *The Magna Charta,* Philadelphia, 1900.
11. Andrew Lang (trans.), *Aucassin and Nicolote,,* London: David Nutt in the Strand, 1896.
12. *The Decameron of Giovanni Boccaccio,*

trans. by Henry Morley, London: George Routledge, 1895.
13. Henderson, *Op.Cit.*
14. W.W. Sheat (ed.)*The Vision of William Concerning Piers the Plowman in Three Parallel Texts,*, Oxford Univ. Press, 1886. Vol I.
15. E.H. McNeal, *The Conquest of Constantinople Translated from the Old French of Robert of Clari,* New York: Columbia Univ. Press, 1936.
16. *Translations and Reprints. . .* I, 4.

III
RENAISSANCE CIVILIZATION

A. ETHICS

1. In Praise of Folly, Erasmus

Erasmus of Rotterdam (1466-1536) was a leading man of letters whose influence earned him the title "Prince of Humanists." His writings set forth the aim of the Christian humanist which was to improve 16th century society through the use of the classics combined with the ideals of Christianity. Many of the writings of Erasmus urged reform and return to the simple gospel of Jesus.

To this same class of fools belong those who beguile themselves with the silly but pleasing notion that if they look upon a picture or image of St. Christopher,—that huge Polyphemus,—they will not die that day; or that he who salutes an image of St. Barbara with the proper form of address will come back from battle safe. . . .

And what shall I say of those who comfortably delude themselves with imaginary pardons for their sins, and who measure the time in purgatory with an hour glass into years, months, days, hours, with all the precision of a mathematical table?

The trader, the soldier, and the judge think that they can clean up the Augean stable of a limetime, once for all, by sacrificing a single coin from their ill-gotten gains. They flatter themselves that all sorts of perjury, debauchery, drunkenness, quarrels, bloodshed, imposture, perfidy, and treason can be compounded for by contract and so adjusted that, having paid off their arrears, they can begin a new score.

How foolish, too, for religious bodies each to give preference to its particular guardian saint! Nay, each saint has his particular office allotted him, and is addressed each in his special way: the one is called upon to alleviate toothache; that, to aid in childbirth; others, to restore a stolen article, bring rescue to the shipwrecked, or protect cattle,—and so on with the rest, who are much too numerous to mention.

And for what, after all, do men petition the saints except for foolish things? Look at the votive offerings which cover the walls of certain churches and with which you see even the ceiling filled; do you find any one who expresses his gratitude that he has escaped Folly or because he has become a whit wiser? One perhaps was saved from drowning, another recovered when he had been run through by his enemy; another, while his fellows were fighting, ran away with expedition and escaped, through the success; another, on the point of being hanged, escaped, through the aid of some saintly friend of thieves, and lived to relieve a few more of those whom he believed to be overburdened with their wealth. . . .

. . . But what if some odious philosopher should chime in and say, as is quite true: "You will not die badly if you live well. You are redeeming your sins when you add to the sum that you contribute a hearty detestation of evil doers: then you may spare yourself tears, vigils, invocation, fasts, and all that kind of life. You may rely upon any saint to aid you when once you begin to imitate his life."

As for the theologians, perhaps the less said the better on this gloomy and dangerous theme. . . .

St. Paul, they admit, was distinguished for his faith, but nevertheless when he said, "Faith is the substance of things hoped for, the evidence of things not seen," he defined it but inaccurately. He may have excelled in charity, yet he fails to limit and define it with dialectic precision in his first letter to the Corinthians, Chapter XIII. The disciples administered the eucharist reverently, and yet had they been asked about the *terminus a quo* and the *terminus ad quem* of transubstantiation; as to how a body can be in two places at the same time; of the differences which exist between Christ's body in heaven, on the cross, and in the holy wafer; or at what point does transubstantiation occur, since the prayer through which it is effected is, as a *quantitas discreta,* in a state of flux,—asked of these matters the apostles would not have replied with the acuteness with which the followers of Scotus distinguish and define these subtleties.

The apostles knew the mother of Jesus, but who of them could philosophically prove how she was preserved from the sin of Eve, as do our divines? Peter received the keys, and from one who would not commit them to unworthy hands, but whether or not he knew how one could have the key of knowledge without knowledge itself, he certainly never discussed the matter. The apostles baptized, but never taught the formal, material, efficient, or final cause of baptism, nor do they mention delible or indelible characters.

Next to the theologians in their self-satisfaction may be ranked those who are commonly called the religious and the monks, both terms quite wide of the truth, since a good part of them are a long ways from religion, and as for the monks (whose names suggests solitude), they are to be met in every byway.

The greater part of the monks exhibit such confidence in ceremonies and trivial human traditions that one would think a single heaven would scarce suffice as a worthy reward for their merits. They little think that Christ will put them off with a "Who hath required these things at your hands?" and will call them to account only for the stewardship of his legacy of love. One will confidently call attention to his paunch, filled with all kinds of fish; another will pour out a hundred bushels of psalms; a third will enumerate his myriad fastings and will tell how a single meal nearly killed him; a fourth will produce as many ceremonies as would fill seven merchant ships; a fifth will plead that for threescore years he never so much as touched money except he fingered it through double thick gloves; a sixth will bring along his hood so old and nasty that no sailor would venture to protect himself with it. . . . But Christ shall interrupt their boastings: "Woe unto you, scribes and Pharisees! I left you one great precept, but of that alone I hear nothing from you. I told you plainly in my gospel, with no disguising parables, that my Father's kingdom was promised, not for cowls, petitions, and fastings, but for deeds of love. I know them not who rely on their own merits.

When the monks and friars shall hear these things and shall see simple sailors and carters preferred to them, how shall their faces fall as they look at one another!

2. Ninety-five Theses, Luther

Written in Latin and posted on a church door in Wittenberg in 1517, the ninety-five theses set forth Martin Luther's reaction to the preaching of indulgences by the Dominican John Tetzel. Luther felt that the selling of indulgences was harmful to the spiritual life of his parishioners. The ninety-five theses which were soon translated into German and widely circulated may be considered the first public step in the break with Rome and the beginning of the Protestant movement.

In the desire and with the purpose of elucidating the truth, a disputation will be held on the underwritten proposition at Wittenberg, under the presidency of the Reverend Father Martin Luther, Monk of the Order of St. Augustine, Master of Arts and of Sacred Theology, and ordinary Reader of the same in that place, He therefore asks those who cannot be present and discuss the subject with us orally, to do so by letter in their absence. In the name of our Lord Jesus Christ. Amen.

5. The Pope has neither the will nor the power to remit any penalties except those which he has imposed by his own authority, or by that of the canons.

6. The Pope has no power to remit any guilt, except by declaring and warranting it to have been remitted by God: or at most by remitting cases reserved for himself; in which cases, if his power were despised, guilt would certainly remain.

7. Certainly God remits no man's guilt without at the same time subjecting him, humbled in all things, to the authority of his representative the priest.

48. Christians should be taught that the Pope, in granting pardons, has both more need and more desire that devout prayer should be made for him than that the money should be readily paid.

49. Christians should be taught that the Pope's pardons are useful if they do not put their trust in them, but most hurtful if through them they lose the fear of God.

50. Christians should be taught that, if the Pope were acquainted with the exactions of the Preachers of pardons, he would prefer that the Basilica of St. Peter should be burnt to ashes rather than that it should be built up with the skin, flesh, and bones of his sheep.

81. This license in the preaching of pardons makes it no easy thing, even for learned men, to protect the reverence due to the Pope against the calumnies, or at all events, the keen questioning of the laity.

82. As for instance: Why does not the Pope empty Purgatory for the sake of most holy charity and of the supreme necessity of souls—they being the most just of all reasons—if he redeems an infinite number of souls for the sake of that most fatal thing, money, to be spent on building a basilica—this being a very slight reason?

83. Again; why do funeral masses and anniversary masses for the deceased continue, and why does not the Pope return, or permit the withdrawal of, the funds bequeathed for

this purpose, since it is a wrong to pray for those who are already redeemed?

86. Again; why does not the Pope, whose riches are at this day more ample than those of the wealthiest of the wealthy, build the single Basilica of St. Peter with his own money rather than with that of poor believers?

87. Again; what does the Pope remit or impart to those who through perfect contrition have a right to plenary remission and participation?

89. Since it is the salvation of souls, rather than money, that the Pope seeks by his pardons, why does he suspend the letters and pardons granted long ago, since they are equally efficacious?

3. Institutes of the Christian Religion

John Calvin the French born reformer published the first edition of his **Institutes of the Christian Religion** *in 1536. The* **Institutes** *are regarded by many as the foremost orderly and concise synthesis of protestant theology. This work soon established Calvin's reputation and under his leadership Geneva became the center of an international religious movement. (see reading #6)*

Of Original Sin

. . . Original sin, then, may be defined a hereditary corruption and depravity of our nature, extending to all parts of the soul, which first makes us obnoxious to the wrath of God, and then produced in us works which in Scripture are termed works of the flesh. This corruption is repeatedly designated by Paul by the term sin, (Galatians 5:19) while the works which proceed from it, such as adultery, fornication, theft, hatred, murder, revellings, . . . the fruits of sin, though in various passages of Scripture and even by Paul himself, they are also termed sins. The two things, therefore, are to be distinctly observed, viz., that being thus perverted and corrupted in all the parts of our nature, we are, merely on account of such corruption, deservedly condemned by God, to whom nothing is acceptable but righteousness, innocence, and purity. This is not liability for another's fault. For when it is said, that the sin of Adam has made us obnoxious to the justice of God, the meaning is not, that we, who are in ourselves innocent and blameless, are bearing his guilt, but that since by his transgression we are all placed under his curse, he is said to have brought us under obligation. Through him, however, not only has punishment been derived, but pollution instilled, for which punishment is justly due. Hence, those who have defined original sin as the want of the original righteousness which we ought to have had, though they substantially comprehend the whole case, do not significantly enough express its power and energy. For our nature is not only utterly devoid of goodness but so prolific in all kinds of evil, that it can never be idle.

Of Predestination

The covenant of life is not preached equally to all, and among those to whom it is preached, does not always meet with the same reception. This diversity displays the unsearchable depth of the divine judgment, and is without doubt subordinate to God's purpose of eternal election. But if it is plainly owing to the mere pleasure of God that salvation is spontaneously offered to some, while others have no access to it, great and difficult questions immediately arise, questions which are inexplicable, when just views are not entertained concerning election and predestination. We shall never feel persuaded as we ought that our salvation flows from the free mercy of God as its fountain, until we are made acquainted with his eternal election, the grace of God being illustrated by the contrast, viz., that he does not adopt all promiscuously to the hope of salvation, but gives to some what he denies to others. It is plain how greatly ignorance of his principle detracts from the glory of God, and impairs true humility. But though thus necessary to be known, Paul declares that it cannot be known unless God, throwing works entirely out of view, elect those whom he has predestined. His words are, "Even so then as this present time else, there is a remnant according to the election of grace. And if by grace, then it is no more of works: otherwise grace is no more grace. But if it be of works, then it is no more grace: otherwise work is no more work." "(Romans 11:6) If to make it appear that our salvation flows entirely from the good mercy of God, we must be carried back to the origin of election, then those who would extinguish it, wickedly do as much as in them lies to obscure what they ought most loudly to extol, and pluck up humility by the very roots. Paul clearly declares that it is only when the salvation of a remnant is ascribed to gratuitous election, we arrive at the knowledge that God saves whom he wills of his mere good pleasure, and does not pay a debt, a debt which never can be due.

The predestination by which God adopts some to the hope of life, and adjudges others to eternal death, no man who would be thought pious ventures simply to deny; but it is greatly cavilled at, especially by those who make prescience its cause. When we attribute prescience to God, we mean that all things always were, and ever continue, under his eye; that to his knowledge there is not past or future, but all things are present, and indeed so present that it is not merely the idea of them that is before him . . . but that he truly sees and contemplates them as actually under his immediate inspection. This prescience extends to the whole circuit of the world, and to all creatures. By predestination we mean the eternal decree of God, by which he determined with himself whatever he wished to happen with regard to every man. All are not created on equal terms, but some are preordained to eternal life, others to eternal damnation; and, accordingly, as each has been created for one or other of these ends, we say that he has been predestinated to life or to death. . . .

Civil Government

. . . civil government is designed, as long as we live in this world, to cherish and support the external worship of God, to preserve the pure doctrine of religion, to defend the constitution of the Church, to regulate our lives in a manner requisite for the society of men, to form our manners to civil justice, to promote our concord with each other, and to establish general peace and tranquility. . . .

But in the obedience which we have shown to be due to the authority of governors, it is always necessary to make one exception, and that is entitled to our first attention—that it do no seduce us from obedience to Him, to whose will the desires of all kings ought to be subject, to whose decrees all their commands ought to be subject, to whose decrees all their commands ought to yield, to whose majesty all their sceptres ought to submit. And, indeed, how preposterous it would be for us, with a view to satisfy men, to incur the displeasure of God on whose account we yield obedience to Kings! The Lord, therefore, is the King of Kings; who, when he has opened his sacred mouth, is to be heard alone, above all, for all, and before all; in the next place, we are subject to those men who preside over us; but not otherwise than in Him. If they command anything against Him, it ought not to have the least attention; nor, in this case, ought we to pay any regard to all that dignity attached to magistrates; to which no injury is done when it is subjected to the unrivalled and supreme power of God.

4. Catholic Reformation, Council of Trent

The Council of Trent, which met in three stages or Assemblies between 1545-63, was directed by a reformed papacy and is considered the climax of the Catholic or counter reformation because it played a leading role in revitalizing and centralizing the Catholic church. In the area of doctrine the council rejected suggestions of conciliation or compromise and concentrated on restating and reaffirming traditional Catholic teaching with emphasis on the points in dispute with the Protestant movement.

Decree Touching the Opening of the Council

Doth it please you, —unto the praise and glory of the holy and undivided Trinity, Father, and Son, and Holy Ghost; for the increase and exaltation of the Christian faith and religion; for the extirpation of heresies; for the peace and union of the Church; for the reformation of the Clergy and Christian people; for the depression and extinction of the enemies of the Christian name,—to decree and declare that the sacred and general council of Trent do begin, and hath begun?

They answered: It pleaseth us.

Decree Concerning the Edition, and the Use, of the Sacred Books

Moreover, the same sacred and holy Synod,—considering that no small utility may accrue to the Church of God, if it be made known which out of all the Latin editions, now in circulation, of the sacred books, is to be held as authentic,—ordains and declares, that the said old and vulgate edition, which, by the lengthened usage of so many ages, has been approved of in the Church, be . . . held as authentic; and that no one is to dare, or presume to reject it under any pretext whatever.

Furthermore, in order to restrain petulant spirits, It decrees, that no one . . . shall,—in matters of faith, and of morals pertaining to the edification of Christian doctrine . . . presume to interpret the said sacred Scripture contrary to that sense which holy mother Church,—whose it is to judge of the true sense and interpretation of the holy Scriptures,—hath held and doth hold; or even contrary to the unanimous consent of the Fathers; even though such interpretations were never (intended) to be at any time published.

Decree Concerning Original Sin

That our *Catholic faith, without which it is impossible to please God,* may, errors being purged away, continue in its own perfect and spotless integrity . . . following the testimonies of the sacred Scriptures, of the holy Fathers, of the most approved councils, and the judgment and consent of the Church itself, ordains, confesses, and declares these things touching the said original sin:

1. If any one does not confess that the first man, Adam, when he had transgressed the commandment of God in Paradise, immediately lost the holiness and justice wherein he had been constituted; and that he incurred, through the offence of that prevarication, the wrath and indignation of God, and consequently death . . . let him be anathema.

2. If any one asserts, that the prevarication of Adam injured himself alone, and not his posterity; and that the holiness and justice, received of God, which he lost, he lost for himself alone, and not for us also; or that he, being defiled by the sin of disobedience, has only transfused death, and pains of the body, into the whole human race, but not sin also, which is the death of the soul; let him be anathema. . . .

3. If any one asserts, that this sin of Adam . . . is taken away either by the powers of human nature, or by any other remedy than the merit of the *one mediator, our Lord Jesus Christ* . . . or if he denies that the said merit of Jesus Christ is applied, both to adults and to infants, by the sacrament of baptism rightly administered in the form of the Church; let him be anathema. . . .

Decree on the Sacraments in General

Canon I.—If any one saith, that the sacraments not all instituted by Jesus Christ, our Lord; or, that they are more, or less, than seven, to wit, Baptism, Confirmation, the Eurcharist, Penance, Extreme Unction, Order, and Matrimony; or even that any one of these seven is not truly and properly a sacrament; let him be anathema.

Canon IV.—If any one saith, that the sacraments of the New Law are not necessary unto salvation, but superfluous; and that, without them, or without the desire thereof, men obtain of God, through faith alone, the grace of justification . . . let him be anathema.

Canon IX.—If any one saith, that, in the three sacraments, Baptism, to wit, Confirmation, and Order, there is not imprinted in the soul a character, that is, a certain spiritual and indelible sign, on account of which they cannot be repeated; let him be anathema.

Canon XII.—If any one saith, that a minister, being in mortal sin, —if so be that he observe all the essentials which belong to the effecting, or conferring of, the sacrament,—neither effects, nor confers the sacrament; let him be anathema. . . .

Decree Concerning the Most Holy Sacrament of the Eucharist

. . . And because that Christ, our Redeemer, declared that which He offered under the species of bread to be truly His own body, therefore has it ever been a firm belief in the Church of God, and his Holy Synod doth now declare it anew, that, by the consecration of the bread and of the wine, a conversion is made of the whole substance of the bread into the substance of the body of Christ our Lord, and of the whole substance of the wine into the substance of His blood; which conversion is, by the holy Catholic Church, suitably and properly called Transubstantiation.

Decree on Reformation

. . . And forasmuch as, though the habit does not make the monk, it is nevertheless needful that clerics always wear a dress suitable to their proper order, that by the decency of their outward apparel they may show forth the inward correctness of their morals . . . for this cause, all ecclesiastical persons, howsoever exempted, who are either in sacred orders or in possession of any manner of dignities, personates, or other offices, or benefices ecclesiastical; if, after having been admonished by their own bishop, even by a public edit, they shall not wear a becoming clerical dress, suitable to their order and dignity, and in conformity with the ordinance and mandate of the said bishop, they nay, and ought to be, compelled thereunto, by suspension from their orders, office, benefice, and from the fruits, revenues, and proceeds of the said benefices; and also, if, after having been once rebuked, they offend again herein (they are to be coerced) even by deprivation of the said offices and benefices. . . .

Canon II.—If any one saith, that by those words, *Do this* for the commemoration of me, . . . Christ did not institute the apostles priests; or, did not ordain that they, and other priests should offer His own body and blood; let him be anathema.

Canon III.—If any one saith, that the sacrifice of the mass is only a sacrifice of praise and of thanksgiving; or, that it is a bare commemoration of the sacrifice consummated on the cross, but not a propitiatory sacrifice; or, that it profits him only who receives; and that it ought not to be offered for the living and the dead for sins, pains, satisfactions, and other necessities; let him be anathema.

On the Sacrament of Matrimony

Canon IX.—If any one saith, that clerics constituted in sacred orders, or Regulars, who have solemnly professed chastity, are able to contract marriage, and that being contracted it is valid, notwithstanding the ecclesiastical law, or vow; and that the contrary is nothing else than to condemn marriage; and, that all who do not feel that they have the gift of chastity, even though they have made a vow thereof, may contract marriage; let him be anathema. . . .

B. LAW

5. Peasant Demands

In an age when the Humanists were emphasizing the individual, with the break up of the Catholic Church, the end of knighthood, and the emerging of the middle class; the peasants attempted to break the bonds of serfdom. Although moderate by our standards, it was enough to cause condemnation by the German leaders, including Martin Luther; and a blood-bath in order to crush such "radicalism."

Peace to the Christian reader and the grace of God through Christ:

There are many evil writings put forth of late which take occasion, on account of the assembling of the peasants, to cast scorn upon the gospel, saying, "Is this the fruit of the new teaching, that no one should obey but that all should everywhere rise in revolt, and rush together to reform, or perhaps destroy altogether, the authorities, both ecclesiastic and lay?" The articles below shall answer these godless and criminal fault-finders, and serve, in the first place, to remove the reproach from the word of God, and, in the second place, to give a Christian excuse for the disobedience or even the revolt of the entire peasantry. . . .

The First Article. First, it is our humble petition and desire, as also our will and resolution, that in the future we should have power and authority so that each community should choose and appoint a pastor, and that we should have the right to depose him should he conduct himself improperly.

The Second Article . . . we are ready and willing to pay the fair tithe of grain . . . . We will that for the future our church provost, whomsoever the community may appoint, shall gather and receive this tithe. From this he shall give to the pastor, elected by the whole community, a decent and sufficient maintenance for him and his. . . . What remains over shall be given to the poor of the place. . . .

The Third Article . . . . We therefore take it for granted that you will release us from serfdom as true Christians, unless it should be shown us from the gospel that we are serfs.

The Seventh Article . . . . The lord should no longer try to force more services or other dues from the peasant without payment, but permit the peasant to enjoy his holding in peace and quiet. . . .

The Eighth Article . . . we are greatly burdened by holdings which cannot support the rent exacted from them . . . we ask that the lords may appoint persons of honor to inspect these holdings, and fix a rent in accordance with justice. . . .

The Tenth Article . . . we are aggrieved by the appropriation by individuals of meadows and fields which at one time belonged to a community. These we will take again into our own hands. It may, however, happen that the land was rightfully purchased. When, however, the land has unfortunately been purchased in this way, some brotherly arrangement should be made according to circumstances.

Conclusion . . . . It is our conclusion and final resolution that if any one or more of the articles here set forth should not be in agreement with the word of God, as we think they are, such article we will willingly retract. . . . Or if articles should now be conceded to us that are hereafter discovered to be unjust, from that hour they shall be dead and null and without force. . . .

6. City of God on Earth, Ordinances of Geneva

The desire of the Calvinists to create a "City of God" on earth led to the passage of strict laws to protect the morals of the people. These concepts passed into the Calvinist-dominated states, surviving in the United States as the "blue laws."

The office of the elders [presbyters] is to watch over the conduct of every individual, to admonish lovingly those whom they see doing wrong or leading an irregular life. When there is need, they should lay the matter before the body deputed to inflict paternal discipline, of which they are members. As the Church is organized, it is best that the elders be chosen, two from the small council, four from the council of sixty, and six from the council of two hundred; they should be men of good life and honest, without reproach and beyond suspicion, above all God-fearing and endowed with spiritual prudence. And they should be chosen that they be distributed in each quarter of the city, so that they can have an eye on everything. . . .

The elders . . . shall assemble once a week with the ministers, namely Thursday morning, to see if there be any disorders in the Church and discuss together such remedies as shall be necessary. . . . If any one shall . . . refuse to appear before them, it shall be their duty to inform the council, so that it may supply a remedy.

Blasphemy. Whoever shall have blasphemed, swearing by the body or by the blood of our Lord, or in similar manner, he shall be made to kiss the earth for the first offence; for the second to pay 5 sous, and for the third 6 sous, and for the last offence to be put on the pillory for one hour.

Drunkenness. That no one shall invite another to drink under penalty of 3 sous.

That taverns shall be closed during the sermon, under penalty that the tavern-keeper shall pay 3 sous, and whoever may be found therein shall pay the same amount.

If any one be found intoxicated he shall pay for the first offence 3 sous and shall be remanded to the consistory; for the second offence he shall be held to pay the sum of 6 sous, and for the third 10 sous and be put in prison.

Songs and Dances. If anyone sing immoral, dissolute or outrageous songs, or dance the *virollet* or other dance, he shall be put in prison for three days and then sent to the consistory.

Usury. That no one shall take upon interest or profit more than five per cent, upon penalty of confiscation of the principal and of being condemned to make restitution as the case may demand.

Games. That no one shall play at any dissolute game or at any game whatsoever it may be, neither for gold nor silver nor for any excessive stake, upon penalty of 5 sous and forfeiture of [the] stake played for.

7. A Declaration of Independence, Holland

Although it would be another century before John Locke would present his natural right concept—that a group had the right to remove a distasteful ruler, the Netherlands in the sixteenth century, declared its independence, by stating the King of Spain, because of his actions, had lost his right to be their monarch.

As 'tis apparent to all that a prince is constituted by God to be ruler of a people, to defend them from oppression and violence as the shepherd his sheep: and whereas God did not create the people slaves to their prince, to obey his commands, whether right or wrong, but rather the prince for the sake of the subjects (without which he could be no prince), to govern them according to equity, to love and support them as a father his children or a shepherd his flock, and even at the hazard of life and preserve them. And when he does not behave thus, but, on the contrary, oppresses them, seeking opportunities to infringe their ancient customs and privileges, exacting from them slavish compliance, then he is no longer a prince, but a tyrant, and the subjects are to consider him in no other view. And particularly when this is done deliberately, unauthorized by the states, they may not only disallow his authority, but legally proceed to the choice of another prince for their defense. This is the only method left for subjects whose humble petitions and remonstrances could never soften their prince or dissuade him from his tyrannical proceedings; and this is what the law of nature dictates for the defense of liberty, which we ought to transmit to posterity, even at the hazard of our lives.

So, having no hope of reconciliation, and finding no other remedy, we have, agreeable to the law of nature in our own defense, and for maintaining the rights, privileges, and liberties of our countrymen, wives, and children, and latest posterity from being enslaved by the Spaniards, been constrained to renounce allegiance to the King of Spain, and pursue such methods as appear to us most likely to secure our ancient liberties and privileges. Know all men by these presents that, being reduced to the last extremity, as above mentioned, we have unanimously and deliberately declared, and do by these presents declare, that the King of Spain has forfeited, *ipso jure,* all hereditary right to the sovereignty of those countries, and are determined for henceforward not to acknowledge his sovereignty, nor any act of his relating to the domains of the Low Countries, or make use of his name as prince, nor suffer others to do it.

C. SOCIETY

8. Advice to a Teenage Cardinal

This reading concerns the advice of a father to his son. Lorenzo the Magnificient, the famous Renaissance ruler and patron, purchased the position of cardinal for his teenage son Giovanni, who was destined to become Pope Leo X. Here we gain some insight into the do's and don't's of Renaissance social behavior and etiquette.

You are not only the youngest cardinal in the college, but the youngest person that was ever raised to that rank; and you ought therefore to be the most vigilant and unassuming, not giving others occasion to wait for you, either in the chapel, the consistory or upon deputations. You will soon get a sufficient insight into the manners of your brethren. With those of less respectable character converse not with too much intimacy . . . for the sake of public opinion. Converse on general topics with all. On public occasions let your equipage and address be rather below than above mediocrity. A handsome and a well-ordered family will be preferable to a great retinue and a splendid residence. Endeavor to live with regularity, and gradually to bring your expenses within those bounds which in a new establishment cannot perhaps be expected. Silk and jewels are not suitable for persons in your station. Your taste will be better shown in the acquisition of a few elegant remains of antiquity, or in the collecting of handsome books, and by your attendants being learned and well-bred rather than numerous. Invite others to your house oftener than you receive invitations. Practice neither too frequently. Let your own food be plain, and ake sufficient exercise, for those who wear your habit are soon liable, without great caution, to contract infirmities. The station of a cardinal is not less secure than elevated; on which account those who arrive at it too frequently become negligent; conceiving their object is attained and that they can preserve it with little trouble. This idea is often injurious to the life and character of those who entertain it. Be attentive therefore to your conduct, and confide in others too little rather than too much. . . .

9. Corruption Among the Clergy, Savanarola

While the previous reading hinted at much of the wealth and splendor that surrounded the Renaissance Church, this selection reflects the discontent felt by some clerics towards this worldliness within the Church. Girolama Savanarola (1454-1498) called for a return to the principles of humility and simplicity within the Catholic Church. Can Savanarola be compared to any religious figures of today?

See, how in these days prelates and preachers are chained to the earth by love of earthly things; the cure of souls is no longer their concern; they are content with the receipt of revenue; the preachers for the pleasure of princes; to be praised and magnified by them. . . . And they have done worse than this, inasmuch as they have not only destroyed the Church of God, but built up another after their own fashion. This is the new Church . . . built of sticks, namely, of Christians dry as tinder for the fires of hell. . . . Go thou to Rome and throughout Christendom; in the mansions of the great prelates and great lords, there is no concern save for poetry and the oratorical art. Go thither and see, thou shalt find them all with books of the humanities in their hands, and telling one another that they can guide men's souls by means of Virgil, Horace, and Cicero. Wouldst thou see how the Church is ruled by the hands of astrologers? And there is no prelate nor great lord that hath not intimate dealings with some astrologer. . . .

But in this temple of theirs there is one thing that delighteth us much. This is that all therein is painted and gilded. Thus our Church hath many fine outer ceremonies for the solemnization of ecclesiastical rites, grand vestments, and numerous draperies, with gold and silver candlesticks, and so many chalices. . . . There thou seest the great prelates with splendid mitres of gold and precious stones on their heads, and silver crosiers in hand; there they stand at the altar, decked with fine copes and stoles of brocade, chanting those beautiful vespers and masses very slowly, and with so many grand ceremonies, so many organs and choristers, that thou art struck with amazement. . . .

[But earlier Christians] . . . had fewer gold mitres and fewer chalices, for, indeed, what few they possessed were broken up to relieve the needs of the poor; whereas our prelates, for the sake of obtaining chalices, will rob the poor of their sole means of support. . . . In the primitive church the chalices were of wood, the prelates of gold; in these days, the Church hath chalices of gold and prelates of wood. These have introduced devilish games among us; they have no belief in God, and jeer at the mysteries of our faith! What doest Thou, O Lord? Why dost thou slumber? Arise, and come to deliver Thy Church from the hands of the devils, from the hands of tyrants, the hands of iniquitous prelates.

10. The Parisians, Rabelais

Francois Rabelais (1494?-1553), French humanist and satirist, was most famous for his literary works of **Gargantua** *and* **Pantagruel**. *This brief selection provides us with a glimpse into the turbulent life among the sixteenth century urban masses. Are there any similarities to contemporary urban life to be found in this reading?*

". . . for the people of Paris are so sottish, so badot, so foolish and fond by nature, that a juggler, a carrier of indulgences, a pack-horse, or a mule with cymbals, or tinkling bells, a blind fiddler in the middle of a cross lane, shall draw a greater confluence of people together, than an Evangelical preacher."

". . . [Parisians] being, as you know, upon any slight occasion so ready to uproars and insurrections, that foreign nations wonder at the patience of the kings of France who do not by good justice restrain them from such tumultuous courses . . . ."

11. Pride of the Artisan, Cellini

One of the characteristics of the Renaissance spirit was individual pride, which conflicted with the concept of Christian humility. In this selection from his **Autobiography,** *Benevenuto Cellini (1500-71) reflected the thoughts of a Renaissance man. What evidence did Cellini use to measure his work?*

It was the custom at that epoch to wear little golden medals, upon which every nobleman or man of quality had some device or fancy of his own engraved; and these were worn in the cap. Of such pieces I made very many, and found them extremely difficult to work. . . . The admirable craftsman Caradosso . . . used to make such ornaments; and as there were more than one figure on each piece, he asked at least a hundred gold crowns for his fee. This being so—not, however, because his prices were so high, but because he worked so slowly—I began to be employed by certain noblemen, for whom, among other things, I made a medal in competition with that great artist, and it had four figures, upon which I had expended an infinity of labour. These men of quality, when they compared my piece with that of the famous Caradosso, declared that mine was by far the better executed and more beautiful, and bade me ask what I liked as the reward of my trouble; for since I had given them such perfect satisfaction, they wished to do the like by me. I replied that my greatest reward and what I most desired was to have rivalled the master pieces of so eminent an artist. . . .

12. Acceptance of Black Magic, Cellini

Although the Renaissance brought about many changes within Western European society and man, superstition, ignorance, and fear nevertheless persisted. This selection shows that a Renaissance artist could believe in black magic. Not only that, but Cellini reported how he saw the Roman Coliseum "all full of devils." How do we explain Cellini's report of events?

It happened . . . that I became intimate with a Sicilian priest, who was a man of very elevated genius and well instructed in both Latin and Greek letters. In the course of conversation one day we led to talk about the art of necromancy; apropos of which I said: "Throughout my whole life I have had the most intense desire to see or learn something of this art." Thereto the priest replied: "A stout soul and a steadfast must the man have who sets himself to such an enterprise." I answered that of strength and steadfastness of soul I should have enough and to spare, provided I found the opportunity. Then the priest said: "If you have the heart to dare it, I will amply satisfy your curiosity."

The priest one evening made his preparations, and bade me find a comrade, or not more than two. I invited Vincenzio Romoli . . . and the priest took with him a native of Pistoja, who also cultivated the black art. We went together to the Coliseum; and there the priest, having arrayed himself in necromancer's robes, began to describe circles on the earth with the finest ceremonies that can be imagined. I must say that he had to bring precious perfumes and fire, and also drugs of fetid odour. When the preliminaries were completed, he made the entrance into the circle; and taking us by the hand, introduced us one by one inside it. Then he assigned our several functions; to the necromancer, his comrade, he gave the pentacle to hold; the other two of us had to look after the fire and the perfumes; and then he began his incantations. This lasted more than an hour and a half; when several legions appeared, and the Coliseum was all full of devils.

13. Nobility at Home, Castiglione

It is very difficult for contemporary Americans to imagine an existence without many of the luxuries such as radio or television that we take for granted. This reading shows us how members of the Italian nobility entertained themselves at home in the evening. What do you think the nonnobles did for entertainment?

. . . I say that the custom of all the gentlemen of the house was to betake themselves to the Duchess immediately after supper; there, along with other delightful entertainment, music, and dancing which went on continuously, puzzling questions were sometimes propounded, sometimes certain ingenious games were devised at the discretion of one or another person, in which beneath various veils the members of the company many times disclosed their thoughts symbolically to this or that person, as it pleased them. Sometimes other debates arose on various topics, or again sharp raillery was exchanged in lively repartee; often "devices," as we call them today, were invented. Here then a wonderful delight was derived from discussions of this sort, the house being filled . . . with men of noblest wit. . . .

D. ECONOMICS

14. Revenues of Renaissance Rulers

This inventory consists of two lists: (1) waning horsemen, and (2) reduced monetary funds. Wars had wrought economic decline of extraordinary proportion—especially when compared with the usual picture of Renaissance glitter, glow and prosperity.

Income of all the Christian powers and what they are able to do. The king of France with all his force and the feudal services of princes, dukes, marquises, counts, barons, knights, bishops, abbots, canons, priests, and citizens, can in his own country raise 30,000 horsemen skilled in arms. If desiring to send them out of the country the said realm could not, since the costs would be doubled, send more than 15,000 horse. Before the war with their own countrymen, it could have raised 100,000 for that war destroyed both Church and revenues. In the total therefore 15,000 horse. The king of

England with the power of his revenues and the feudal services of princes and others as above could, paying them every month, raise at home 30,000 horsemen skilled in arms. In making the test of war these powers are equal. They have always been powerful in their undertakings. And if one of these forces had been greater than the other, one would have been destroyed. The English were overcome, after the division occurred in England, and they could not make provision for their forces. This was before 1414. They had 40,000 horse. Wars have weakened these countries, their men and their revenues, so that now wishing to send a force out of the country it is agreed that they have the half, i.e., 15,000 horsemen. The king of Scotland is lord of a great country, and of a people of so great poverty that he would not be able to maintain with his revenues and the taxes and dues of the clergy and laity, 10,000 horsemen skilled in arms in his own country; outside of the country on account of the great cost, 5000 horse. The king of Norway who is lord of a great country, and a people equally poor could not maintain at home with his revenues and the taxes and dues of clergy and laity 10,000 horsemen skilled in arms, abroad 5000 horse. The king of Spain with all his revenues and feudal dues of clergy and laity, with all his horces 30,000 horsemen skilled in arms. In 1414 he paid for 20,000. Wishing to maintain them out of the country at double cost they would be 15,000 horsemen.

The Pope with all his revenues of his States of the Church, and with the profits of churches which he receives, was able in 1414 to raise 8000 horsemen; at present at home 6000 horsemen, abroad 3000.

All Germany with the lords temporal and spiritual, the free and the other cities, north and south Germany, and the Emperor who is German, can raise with all their resources and revenues 60,000 horsemen at home and 30,000 abroad. The king of Hungary, with all the dukes, lords, princes, barons, prelates, clergy and laity, and with all his resources and revenues can raise at home 80,000 horsemen, abroad 40,000. The grand master of Prussia with all his revenues, 30,000 horsemen. In 1414 he had 50,000. But war has weakened him. Abroad 15,000 horsemen.

Power of the Infidel Monarchs. The Turk can in all his dominions raise 40,000 horsemen, valiant men to defend him against the Christians. The Caraman with all his power can raise at home 60,000 horsemen, abroad 30,000. Ussun Cassan with all his power can raise at home 20,000 horsemen in the service of Mahomet, abroad 10,000. The Caraifan with all his resources at home 20,000, abroad 10,000. Tamerlane with all his Tartar power can raise at home 1,000,000 horsemen, abroad 500,000. The king of Tunis, of Granada and the other cities of Barbary who have galleys and boats to the injury of Christians, at home are 100,000 horsemen, abroad 50,000.

Revenues of some Christian princes in the year 1423. The king of France in the year 1414 had 2,000,000 ducats ordinary revenues. But the wars which have continued for forty years have reduced the ordinary revenues to 1,000,000 ducats. The king of England had 2,000,000 ducats ordinary revenue. The continued wars have desolated the island. At the present time he has 700,000 ducats revenue. The king of Spain had in 1410, 3,000,000 ducats ordinary revenue, but the continued wars have reduced it to 800,000 ducats.

Florence in 1424 had a revenue of 400,000 ducats. But since then, through the great wars it is reduced to 200,000 ducats. The pope, though formerly he had none, has 400,000 ducats ordinary revenue.

15. Book of Husbandry (1523), Fitzherbert

Fitzherbert has reduced farming (husbandry) to some of its fundamentals. His grasp of these elements is convincing, and his hortatory advice still has versimilitude.

The most general living that husbands can have is by ploughing and sowing of their corn and rearing or breeding their cattle; and not the one without the other. Then is the plough the most necessariest instrument that a husband can occupt, wherefore it is convenient to know how a plough should be made. . . .

It is to be known whether is better a plough of horses or a plough of oxen, and therein, me seems, ought to be made a distinction. For in some places an ox plough is better than a horse plough, and some places a horse plough is better. . . . Oxen will plough in tough clay and upon hilly ground, whereas horses will stand still. . . . Horses will go faster than oxen on even ground or light ground, and quicker in carriages, but they be far more costly to keep in winter. For they must have both hay and corn to eat, and straw for litter; they must be well shod on all four feet, and the gear that they shall draw with is more costly than for the oxen, and shorter while it will last. And the oxen will eat but straw and a little hay, the which is not half the cost that horses must have, and they have no shoes as horses have. And if any sorance come to the horse (wax old, bruised, or blind), then he is little worth. And if any sorance come to an ox (wax old, bruised, or blind) . . . he may be fed and then he is mans meat and as good ox better than ever he was. And the horse, when he dies, is but carrion. And therefore me seems, all things considered, the plough of oxen is much more profitable than the plough of horses. . . .

And husband cannot well thrive by his corn without he has other cattle, nor by his cattle without corn; for else he shall be a buyer, borrower or beggar; and . . . sheep in my opinion is the most profitablest cattle that a man can have. . . .

A shepherd should not go without his dog, his sheep-hook, a pair of shears, and his tax-box either with him or ready at his sheep-fold. And he must teach his dog to bark when he would have him, to run when he would have him, and to leave running when he would have him; or else he is not a cunning shepherd. The dog must learn it when he is a whelp, or else it will not be; for it is hard to make an old dog to stoop. . . .

Now, thou husband that hast both horses and mares, beasts and sheep, it were necessary also that thou have both swine and bees. For it is an old saying: he that has both sheep, swine and bees, sleep he, wake he, he may thrive. And that saying is because that they be those things that most profit rises [from] in shortest space with the least cost. . . .

16. Draft of a Poor Law (1536), William Marshall

William Marshall's plea, preface, and balanced explanation for a "Poor Law" should prove to be both an eye opener regarding earlier socioeconomic sophistication, and an embarrassment concerning today's lack of understanding to the point of misunderstanding.

Forasmuch as the king's majesty has full and perfect notice that there be within this his realm as well a right great multitude of strong valiant beggars, vagabonds and idle persons of both kinds, men and women, which though they might well labour for their living if they would will not yet put themselves to it as divers other of his true and faithful subjects do, but give themselves to live idly by begging and procuring of alms of the people, to the high displeasure of Almighty God, hurt of their own souls, evil example of others, and to the great hurt of the commonwealth of this realm; as also divers other old, sick, lame, feeble and impotent persons not able to labour for their living but are driven of necessity to procure the alms and charity of the people. And his highness has perfect knowledge that some of them have fallen into such poverty only of the visitation of God through sickness and other casualties, and some through their own default, whereby they have come finally to that point that they could not labour for any part of their living but of necessity are driven to live wholly by the charity of the people. And some have fallen to such misery through the default of their masters which have put them out of service in time of sickness and left them wholly without relief and comfort. And some be fallen thereto through default of their friends which in youth have brought them up in overmuch pleasure and idleness, and instructed them not in anything wherewith they might in age get their living. And some have set such as have been under their rule to procure their living by open begging even from childhood, so that they never knew any other way of living but only by begging. And so for lack of good oversight in youth many live in great misery in age. And some have come to such misery through their own default, as through sloth, pride, negligence, falsehood and such other ungraciousness, whereby their masters, lovers and friends have been driven to forsake them and finally no man would take them to any service; whereby they have in process of time lain in the open streets and fallen to utter desolation. And divers other occasions have brought many to such poverty which were very long to rehearse here. But whatsoever the occasion be, charity requires that some way be taken to help and succour them that be in such necessity and also to prevent that others shall not hereafter fall into like misery. Therefore his highness, of his most blessed and godly disposition, like a virtuous price and gracious head regarding as well the maintenance of the commonwealth of his realm, the good governance of his people and subjects being the members of his body, as the relief of the poor, wretched and miserable people whereof be a great multitude in this his realm, and the redress and avoiding of all valiant beggars and idle persons within the same . . . has by the advice of the lords spiritual and temporal and the commons in this present Parliament assembled . . . provided certain remedies as well for the help and relief of such idle, valiant beggars as has been before remembered, as of such poor and miserable people as be before rehearsed, in manner and form following. . . .

17. Early Mercantilism, Thomas Mun

Thomas Mun obviously had a comprehensive knowledge of, and a persuasive series of arguments for mercantilism. What arguments can be given against mercantilism either contemporary with his writings or now?

The ordinary means therefore to encrease our wealth and treasure is by *Forraign Trade*, wherein we must ever observe this rule: to sell more to strangers yearly than we consume of theirs in value. . . .

The revenue or stock of a Kingdom by which it is provided of Forraign wares is either *Natural* or *Artificial.* The Natural wealth is so much only as can be spared from our own use and necessities to be exported unto strangers. The Artificial consists in our manufactures and industrious trading with forraign commodities, concerning which I will set down such particulars as may serve for the cause we have in hand.

1. First, although this Realm be already exceeding rich by nature, yet might it be much encreased by laying the waste grounds (which are infinite) into such employments as should no way hinder the present revenues of other manured lands, but hereby to supply our selves and prevent the importations of Hemp, Flax, Cordage, Tobacco, and divers other things which we now fetch from strangers to our great impoverishing.

2. We may likewise diminish our importations, if we would soberly refrain from excessive consumption of forraign wares in our diet and rayment, with such often change of fashions as is used, so much the more to encrease the waste and charge; which vices at this present are more notorious amongst us than in former ages. . . .

3. In our exportations we must not only regard our own superfluities, but also we must consider our neighbours necessities, that so upon the wares which they cannot want, nor yet be furnished thereof elsewhere, we may (besides the vent of the Materials) gain so much of the manufacture as we can, and also endeavour to sell them dear, so far forth as the high price cause not a less vent in the quantity. But the superfluity of our commodities which strangers use, may also have the same from other Nations, or may abate their vent by the use of some such like wares from other places, and with little inconvenience; we must in this case strive to sell as cheap as possible we can, rather than to lose the utterance of such wares. . . .

4. The value of our exportations likewise may be much advanced when we perform it ourselves in our own Ships for then we get not only the price of our wares as they are worth here, but also the Merchants gains, the changes of ensurance, and fraight to carry them beyond the seas. . . .

6. The Fishing in his Majesties seas of *England, Scotland,* and *Ireland* is our natural wealth, and would cost nothing but labour, which the *Dutch* bestow willingly, and thereby draw yearly a great profit to themselves by serving many places of Christendom with our fish. . . .

12. Lastly, in all things we must endeavour to make the most we can of our own, whether it be *Natural* or *Artificial.*

E. SOURCES FOR PART III

1. Erasmus, *In Praise of Folly,* in James H. Robinson (ed.), *Readings in European History,* Boston: Ginn & Co., 1906.
2. *Translation and Reprints . . .,* II, 6.
3. John Calvin, *Institutes of the Christian Religion,* trans. by Henry Beveridge, Edinburgh: 1845.
4. Philip Schall (ed.), *The Creeds of Christendom,* New York: Harper & Bros., 1877.
5. James H. Robinson, *Op. Cit.*
6. *Translations and Reprints . . .,* III, 3.
7. Oliver J. Thatcher (ed.), *The Library of Original Sources,* Milwaukee: Univ. Research Extension Co., 1907. Vol. V.

8. M. Whitcomb (ed.), *A Literary Source-book of the Italian Renaissance,* Philadelphia: 1900.
9. P. Villari (ed.), *Life and Times of Girolamo Savonarola,* London: 1899
10. Rebelais, *Garantua and Pantagruel,* Paris: 1876.
11. *The Life of Benvenuto Cellini Written by Himself,* New York: Brentano's, [1906].
12. *Ibid.*
13. Baldassari Castiglione, *The Book of the Courtier,* trans. by Sir Thomas Hobby, London: 1561. Spellings updated.
14. *Translations and Reprints . . .,* III, 2.
15. Sir Anthony Fitzherbert, *The Boke of Husbandry,* London: 1523.
16. From British Museum, Royal MS 18. c. vi.
17. Thomas Mun, *England's Treasure by Foreign Trade,* London: The Macmillan Co., 1895.

IV

ENLIGHTENED CIVILIZATION

A. ETHICS

1. Religion and Liberty, Spinoza

Baruch Spinoza (1632.1677) who wrote in Holland was regarded as a radical because of his critical views towards tradition and organized religion. His philosophy and his support of pantheism led to his ostracism by the Jewish community of Amsterdam. His plea for religious toleration in Holland was written in 1670.

Preface

Men would never be superstitious, if they could govern all their circumstances by set rules, or if they were always favoured by fortune: but being frequently driven into straits where rules are useless, and being often kept fluctuating pitiably between hope and fear by the uncertainty of fortune's greedily coveted favours, they are consequently, for the most part, very prone to credulity. The human mind is readily swayed this way or that in times of doubt, especially when hope and fear are struggling for the mastery, though usually it is boastful, over-confident, and vain. . . .

Superstition, then, is engendered, preserved, and fostered by fear. Very numerous examples of a like nature might be cited, clearly showing the fact, that only while under the dominion of fear do men fall a prey to superstition; that all the portents ever invested with the reverence of misguided religion are mere phantoms of dejected and fearful minds; and lastly, that prophets have most power among the people, and are most formidable to rulers, precisely at those times when the state is in most peril.

The origin of superstition above given affords us a clear reason for the fact, that it comes to all men naturally, though some refer its rise to a dim notion of God, universal to mankind, and also tends to show, that it is no less inconsistent and variable than other mental hallucinations and emotional impulses, and further that it can only be maintained by hope, hatred, anger, and deceit; since it springs, not from reason, but solely from the more powerful phases of emotion. . . . For, as the mass of mankind remains always at about the same pitch of misery, it never assents long to any one remedy, but it always best pleased by a novelty which has not yet proved illusive.

This element of inconsistency has been the cause of many terrible wars and revolutions; for, as Curtius well says . . . : "The mob has no ruler more potent than superstition," and is easily led, on the plea of religion, at one moment to adore its kings as gods, and anon to execrate and abjure them as humanity's common bane. Immense pains have therefore been taken to counteract this evil by investing religion, whether true or false, with such pomp and ceremony, that it may rise superior to every shock, and be always observed with studious reverence by the whole people. . . .

But if, in despotic statecraft, the supreme and essential mystery be to hoodwink the subjects, and to mask the fear which keeps them down, with the specious garb of religion, so that men may fight as bravely for slavery as for safety, and count it not shame but highest honour to risk their blood and their lives for the vainglory of a tyrant; yet in a free state no more mischievous expedient could be planned or attempted. Wholly repugnant to the general freedom are such devices as enthralling men's minds with prejudices, forcing their judgment, or employing any of the weapons of quasireligious sedition; indeed, such seditions only spring up, when law enters the domain of speculative thought, and opinions are put on trial and condemned on the same footing as crimes, while those who defend and follow them are sacrificed, not to public safety, but to their opponents' hatred and cruelty.

Now, seeing that we have the rare happiness of living in a republic, where everyone's judgment is free and unshackled, where each may worship God as his conscience dictates, and where freedom is esteemed before all things dear and precious, I have believed that I should be undertaking no ungrateful or unprofitable task, in demonstrating that not only can such freedom be granted without prejudice to the public peace, but also, that without such freedom, piety cannot flourish nor the public peace be secure.

Such is the chief conclusion I seek to establish in this treatise; but, in order to reach it, I must first point out the misconceptions which, like scars of our former bondage, still disfigure our notion of religion. . . . As to the order of my treatise I will speak presently, but first I will recount the causes which led me to write.

I have often wondered, that persons who make a boast of professing the Christian religion, namely, love, joy, peace, temperance, and charity of all men, should quarrel with such rancorous animosity, and display daily towards one another such bitter hatred, that this, rather than the virtues they claim, is the readiest criterion of their faith. Inquiry into the cause of this anomaly leads me unhesitatingly to ascribe it to the fact, that the ministries of the Church are regarded by the masses merely as dignities, her offices as posts of emolument—in short, popular religion may be summed up as respect for ecclesiastics. The spread of this misconception inflamed every worthless fellow with an intense desire to enter holy orders, and thus the love of diffusing God's religion degenerated into sordid avarice and ambition. Every church became a theatre, which orators, instead of church teachers, harangued, caring not to instruct the people, but striving to attract admiration, to bring opponents to public scorn, and to preach only novelties and paradoxes, such as would tickle the ears of their congregation. This state of things necessarily stirred up an amount of controversy, envy, and hatred, which no lapse of time could appease; so that we can scarcely wonder that of the old religion nothing survives but its outward forms . . . and that faith has become a mere compound of credulity and prejudices. . . .

Furthermore, if any Divine light were in then, it would appear from their doctrine. I grant that they are never tired of professing their wonder at the profound mysteries of Holy Writ; still I cannot discover that they teach anything but speculations of Platonists and Aristotelians, to which (in order to save their credit for Christianity) they have made Holy Writ conform; not content to rave with the Greeks themselves, they want to make the prophets rave also; showing conclusively, that never even in sleep have they caught a glimpse of Scripture's Divine nature.

As I pondered over the facts that the light of reason is not only despised, but by many even execrated as a source of impiety, that human commentaries are accepted as divine records, and that credulity is extolled as faith; . . . I determined to examine the Bible afresh in a careful, impartial, and unfettered spirit, making no assumptions concerning it, and attributing to it no doctrines, which I do not find clearly therein set down. I was easily able to conclude, that the authority of the prophets has weight only in matters of morality, and that their speculative doctrines affect us little.

Next I inquired, why the Hebrews were called God's chosen people, and discovering that it was only because God had chosen for them a certain strip of territory, where they might live peaceably and at ease, I learnt that the Law revealed by God to Moses was merely the law of the individual Hebrew state, therefore that it was binding on none but Hebrews, and not even on Hebrews after the downfall of their nation.

Now, as in the whole course of my investigation I found nothing taught expressly by Scripture, which does not agree with our understanding, or which is repugnant thereto, and as I saw that the prophets taught nothing, which is not very simple and easily to be grasped by all, and further, that they clothed their teaching in the style, and confirmed it with the reasons, which would most deeply move the mind of the masses to devotion towards God, I became thoroughly convinced, that the Bible leaves reason absolutely free, that it has nothing in common with philosophy, in fact, that Revelation and Philosophy stand on totally different footings.

Having thus laid bare the bases of belief, I draw the conclusion that Revelation has obedience for its sole object, and therefore, in purpose no less than in foundation and method, stands entirely aloof from ordinary knowledge; each has its separate province, neither can be called the handmaid of the other.

Furthermore, as men's habits of mind differ, so that some more readily embrace one form of faith, some another, for what moves one to pray may move another only to scoff, I conclude, in accordance with what has gone before, that everyone should be free to choose for himself the foundations of his creed, and that faith should be judged only by its fruits; each would then obey God freely with his whole heart, while nothing would be publicly honoured save justice and charity.

Having thus drawn attention to the liberty conceded to everyone by the revealed law of God, I pass on to another part of my subject, and prove that this same liberty can and should be accorded with safety to the state and the magisterial authority—in fact, that it cannot be withheld without great danger to peace and detriment to the community.

2. A Philosophical Dictionary, Voltaire

Francois Marie Arouet (1694-1778) who wrote under the name Voltaire is the best known and most influential writer of the Enlightenment. His works which combine skepticism and rationalism, best exemplify the attitudes of the Age of Reason and stress attacks on superstition and intolerance.

Sect

Every sect, of whatever opinion it may be, is a rallying point for doubt and error. Scotists, Thomists, Realists, Nominalists, Papist, Calvinists, Molinists, and Jansenists, are only warlike appellations.

There is no sect in geometry; we never say: A Euclidian, an Archimedian. When truth is evident, it is impossible to divide people into parties and factions. Nobody disputes that it is broad day at noon.

That part of astronomy which determines the course of the stars, and the return of eclipses, being now known, there is no longer any dispute among astronomers.

It is similar with a small number of truths, which are similarly established; but if you are a Mahometan, as there are many men who are not Mahometans, you may possibly be in error.

What would be the true religion, if Christianity did not exist? That in which there would be no sects; that in which all minds necessarily agreed.

Now, in what doctrine are all minds agreed? In the adoration of one God, and in probity. All the philosophers who have professed a religion have said at all times: "There is a God, and He must be just." Behold then the universal religion, established throughout all time and among all men! The point then in which all agree is true; the systems in regard to which all differ are false.

When Zoroaster, Hermes, Orpheus, Minos, and all the great men say: Let us worship God, and be just, no one laughs; but all the world sneers at him who pretends, that to please God it is proper to die holding a cow by the tail. . . .

Whence this universal assemblage of laughing and hissing from one end of the universe to the other? It must be that the things which all the world derides are not evident truths.

That which my sect teaches me is obscure, I confess it, exclaims a fanatic; and it is in consequence of that obscurity that I must believe it; for it says itself that it abounds in obscurities. My sect is extravagant, therefore it is divine; for how, appearing so insane, would it otherwise have been embraced by so many people. It is precisely like the Koran, which the Sonnites say presents at once the face of an angel and that of a beast. Be not scandalized at the muzzle of the beast, but revere the face of the angel. Thus spoke this madman; but a fanatic of another sect replied to the first fanatic: It is thou who art the beast, and I who am the angel.

Now who will judge this process, and decide between these two inspired personages? The reasonable and impartial man who is learned in a science which is not that of words; the man divested of prejudice, and a lover of truth and of justice; the man, in fine, who is not a beast, and who pretends not to be an angel. . . .

Superstition

The superstitious man is to the knave, what the slave is to the tyrant; nay more—the superstitious man is governed by the fanatic, and becomes a fanatic himself. Superstition, born in Paganism, adopted by Judaism, infected the Church in the earliest ages. All the fathers of the Church, without exception, believed in the power of magic. The Church always condemned magic, but she always believed in it; she excommunicated sorcerers, not as madmen who were in delusion, but as men who really had intercourse with the devils.

At this day, one half of Europe believes that the other half has long been and still is superstitious. The Protestants regard relics, indulgences, macerations, prayers for the dead, holy water, and almost all the rites of the Roman church, as mad superstitions. According to them, superstition consists in mistaking useless practices for necessary ones. Among the Roman Catholics there are some, more enlightened than their forefathers, who have renounced many of these usages formerly sacred; and they defend their adherence to those which they have retained, by saying they are indifferent, and what is indifferent cannot be an evil.

It is then nowhere agreed among Christian societies what superstition is. It is therefore evident that what is the foundation of the religion of one sect, is by another sect regarded as superstitious.

Who shall decide this great cause? Shall not reason? But each sect declares that reason is on its side. Force then will decide, until reason shall have penetrated into a sufficient number of heads to disarm force.

Can there exist a people free from all superstitious prejudices? This is asking, Can there exist a people of philosophers? It is said that there is no superstition in the magistracy of China. It is likely that the magistracy of some towns in Europe will also be free from it. These magistrates will then prevent the superstition of the people from being dangerous. In short, the fewer superstitions, the less fanaticism; and the less fanaticism, the fewer calamities.

Toleration

Of all religions, the Christian ought doubtless to inspire the most toleration, although hitherto the Christians have been the most intolerant of all men. Jesus, having deigned to be born in poverty and lowliness like his brethren, never condescended to practice the art of writing. The Jews had a law written with the greatest minuteness, and we have not a single line from the hand of Jesus. The apostles were divided on many points. St. Peter and St. Barnabas ate forbidden meats with the new stranger Christians, and abstained from them with the Jewish Christians. St Paul reproached them with this conduct; and this same St. Paul, the Pharisee, the disciple of the Pharisee Gamaliel—this same St. Paul, who had persecuted the Christians with fury, and who after breaking with Gamaliel became a Christian himself—nevertheless, went afterwards to sacrifice in the temple of Jerusalem, during his apostolic vacation. For eight days he observed publicly all the ceremonies of the Jewish law which he had renounced; he even added devotions and purifications which were superabundant; he completely Judaized. The greatest apostle of the Christians did, for eight days, the very things for which men are condemned to the stake among a large portion of Christian nations.

When at length some Christians had embraced the dogmas of Plato, and mingled a little philosophy with their religion, which they separated from the Jewish, they insensibly became more considerable, but were always divided into many sects, without there ever having been a time when the Christian church was reunited.

This horrible discord, lasting for so many centuries, is a very striking lesson that we ought mutually to forgive each other's errors: discord is the great evil of the human species, and toleration is its only remedy.

There is nobody who does not assent to this truth, whether meditating cooly in his closet, or examining the truth peaceably with his friends. Why, then, do the same men who in private admit charity, beneficence, and justice, oppose themselves in public so furiously against these virtues? Why!—it is because their interest is their god; because they sacrifice all to that monster whom they adore.

If there is any sect which reminds one of the time of the first Christians, it is undeniably that of the Quakers. The apostles received the spirit. The Quakers receive the spirit. The apostles and disciples spoke three or four at once in the assembly in the third story; the Quakers do as much on the ground floor. Women were permitted to preach, according to St. Paul, and they were forbidden according to the same St. Paul: the Quakeresses preach by virtue of the first permission.

It would be easy to push the parallel farther; it would be still easier to demonstrate how much the Christian religion of our day differs from the religion which Jesus practiced. Jesus was a Jew, and we are not Jews. Jesus abstained from pork, because it is uncleanly, and from habit, because it ruminates and its foot is not cloven; we fearlessly eat pork, because it is not uncleanly for us, and we eat rabbit which has the cloven foot and does not ruminate.

But what! must we all Judaize, because Jesus Judaized all His life? If it were allowed to reason logically in matters of religion, it is clear that we ought all to become Jews, since Jesus Christ, our Saviour, was born a Jew, lived a Jew and died a Jew, and since He expressly said, that he accomplished and fulfilled the Jewish religion. But it is still more clear that we ought mutually to tolerate one another, because we are all weak, irrational, and subject to change and error. A reed prostrated by the wind in the mire—ought it to say to a neighboring reed placed in a contrary direction: Creep after my fashion, wretch, or I will present a request for you to be seized and burned? . . .

3. Reflections of a Deist, Franklin

This selection is from the Autobiography of Benjamin Franklin (1706-90) American printer, scientist, writer and statesman who was familiar with the key ideas of the Enlightenment. The reader may wish to note the central ideas of deism and Franklin's program for self-improvement.

Before I enter upon my public appearance in business, it may be well to let you know the then state of my mind with regard to my principles and morals, that you may see how far those influenced the future of my life. My parents had early given me religious impressions, and brought me through my childhood piously in the Dissenting way. But I was scarce fifteen, when, after doubting by turns of several points, as I found them disputed in the different books I read, I began to doubt of Revelation itself. Some books against Deism fell into my hands; they were said to be the substance of sermons preached at Boyle's Lectures. It happened that they wrought an effect on me quite contrary to what was intended by them; for the arguments of the Deists, which we quoted to be refuted, appeared to me much stronger than the refutations; in short, I soon became a thorough Deist. I began to suspect that this doctrine, tho' it might be true, was not very useful. My London pamphlet, which had for its motto these lines of Dryden:

> "Whatever is is right. Though purblind man
> See but a part o' the chain, the nearest link:
> His eyes not carrying to the equal beam,
> That poises all above;"

and from the attributes of God, his infinite wisdom, goodness and power, concluded that nothing could possibly be wrong in the world, and that vice and virtue were empty distinctions, no such things existing, appeared now not so clever a performance as I once thought it; and I doubted whether some error had not insinuated itself unperceived into my argument, so as to infect all that followed, as is common in metaphysical reasonings.

I grew convinced that *truth, sincerity* and *integrity* in dealings between man and man were of the utmost importance to the felicity of life; and I formed written resolutions, which still remain in my journal book, to practice them ever while I lived. Revelation had indeed no weight with me, as such: but I entertained an opinion that, though certain actions might not be bad *because* they were forbidden by it, or good *because* it commanded them, yet probably these actions might be forbidden *because* they were bad for us, or commanded *because* they were beneficial to us, in their own natures, all the circumstances of things considered. And this persuasion, with the kind hand of Providence, or some guardian angel, or accidental favorable circumstances and situations, or all together preserved me, through this dangerous time of youth. . . .

I had been religiously educated as a Presbyterian; and tho' some of the dogmas of that persuasion, such as *the eternal decrees of God, election, reprobation, etc.,* appeared to me unintelligible, others doubtful, and I early absented myself from the public assemblies of the sect, Sunday being my studying day, I never was without some religious principles. I never doubted, for instance, the existence of the Deity; that he made the world, and governed it by his Providence; that the most acceptable service of God was the doing good to man; that our souls are immortal; and that all crime will be punished, and virtue rewarded, either here or hereafter. These I esteemed the essentials of every religion; and, being to be found in all the religions we had in our country, I respected them all. . . .

This respect to all, with an opinion that the worst had some good effects, induced me to avoid all discourse that might tend to lessen the good pinion another might have of his own religion; and as our province increased in people, and new places of worship were continually wanted, and generally erected by voluntary contribution, my mite for such purpose, whatever might be the sect, was never refused.

It was about this time I conceived the bold and arduous project of arriving at moral perfection. I wished to live without committing any fault at any time; I would conquer all that either natural inclination, custom, or company might lead me into. As I knew, or thought I knew, what was right and wrong, I did not see why I might not always do the one and avoid the other. But I soon found I had undertaken a task of more difficulty than I had imagined. For this purpose I therefore contrived the following method.

In the various enumerations of the moral virtues I had met with in my reading, I found the catalogue more or less numerous, as different writers included more or fewer ideas under the same name. Temperance, for example, was by some confined to eating and drinking, while by others it was extended to mean the moderating every other pleasure, appetite, inclination, or passion, bodily or mental, even to our avarice and ambition. I proposed to myself, for the sake of clearness, to use rather more names, with fewer ideas annexed to each, than a few names with more ideas; and I included under thirteen names of virtues all that at that time occurred to me as necessary or desirable, and annexed to each a short precept, which fully expressed the extent I gave to its meaning. These names of virtues, with their precepts, were:

1. *Temperance.* Eat not to dulness; drink not to elevation.

2. *Silence.* Speak not but what may benefit others or yourself; avoid trifling conversation.

3. *Order.* Let all your things have their places; let each part of your business have its time.

4. *Resolution.* Resolve to perform what you ought; perform without fail what you resolve.

5. *Frugality.* Make no expense but to do good to others or yourself; i.e., waste nothing.

6. *Industry.* Lose no time; be always employed in something useful; cut off all unnecessary actions.

7. *Sincerity.* Use no hurtful deceit; think innocently and justly, and, if you speak, speak accordingly.

8. *Justice.* Wrong none by doing injuries, or omitting the benefits that are your duty.

9. *Moderation.* Avoid extreams; forbear resenting injuries so much as you think they deserve.

10. *Cleanliness.* Tolerate no uncleanliness in body, cloaths, or habitation.

11. *Tranquillity* Be not disturbed at trifles, or at accidents common or unavoidable.

12. *Chastity.* Rarely use venery but for health or offspring, never to dulness, weakness, or the injury of your own or another's peace or reputation.

13. *Humility.* Imitate Jesus and Socrates.

B. LAW

4. Bill of Rights, England—1689

The Enlightenment was an age of accelerated rights for man. In 1688, the English removed James II, whom they considered a tyrant. In order to protect themselves, they made the acceptance of a list of guarantees by William and Mary as prerequisite to offering them the throne. It is interesting also to note, for one of the first times it was the representatives of the people, not the "grace of God" which made the decision.

And whereas the said late king James II having abdicated the government, and the throne being thereby vacant, his Highness the Prince of Orange . . . did . . . cause letters to be written to the Lords Spiritual and Temporal being Protestants, and other letters to the several counties, cities, universities, boroughs . . . for the choosing of such persons to represent them as were of right to be sent to parliament to meet and sit at Westminster upon the two-and-twentieth day of January in the year . . . [1689] in order to such an establishment as that their religion, laws, and liberties might not again be in danger of being subverted; upon which letters elections have been accordingly made.

And thereupon the said Lords Spiritual and Temporal and Commons . . . declare:—

1. That the pretended power of suspending of laws or the execution of laws by regal authority without consent of Parliament is illegal.

2. That the pretended power of dispensing with laws or the execution of laws by regal authority is illegal.

3. That the commission for erecting the late Court of Commissioners for Ecclesiastical Causes and all other Commissions and Courts of like nature, are illegal and pernicious.

4. That levying money for or to the use of the Crown by pretence of prerogative without consent of Parliament for longer time or in other manner than the same is or shall be granted is illegal.

5. That it is the right of the subjects to

petition the King, and all commitments and prosecutions for such petitioning, are illegal.

6. That the raising or keeping a standing army within the kingdom in time of peace unless it be with consent of Parliament, is against law.

7. That the subjects which are Protestants may have arms for their defence suitable to their conditions and as allowed by law.

8. That election of members of Parliament ought to be free.

9. That the freedom of speech and debates or proceedings in Parliament ought not to be impeached or questioned in any court or place out of Parliament.

10. That excessive bail ought not to be required, nor excessive fines imposed, nor cruel and unusual punishments inflicted.

11. That jurors ought to be duly impanellel and returned, and jurors which pass upon men in trials for high treason, ought to be freeholders.

12. That all grants and promises of fines and forfeitures of particular persons before conviction, are illegal and void.

5. Declaration of Rights, France—1789

A hundred years following the English Glorious Revolution, the French rebelled against absolutism. The natural rights which the National Assembly passed is like reading Locke, Rousseau, or the American Declaration of Independence.

The representatives of the French people, organized in National Assembly, considering that ignorance, forgetfulness, or contempt of the rights of man, are the sole causes of the public miseries and of the corruption of governments, have resolved to set forth in solemn declaration the natural, inalienable and sacred rights of man, in order that this declaration, being ever present to all the members of the social body' may unceasingly remind them of their rights and duties; in order that the acts of the legislative power and those of the executive power may be each moment compared with the aim of every political institution and thereby may be more respected: and in order that the demands of the citizens, grounded henceforth upon simple and incontestable principles, may always take the direction of maintaining the constitution and the welfare of all.

In consequence, the National Assembly recognizes and declares, in the presence and under the auspices of the Supreme Being, the following rights of man and citizen.

1. Men are born and remain free and equal in rights. Social distinctions can be based only upon public utility.

2. The aim of every political association is the preservation of the natural and imprescriptible rights of man. These rights are liberty, property, security and resistance to oppression.

3. The source of all sovereignty is essentially in the nation; no body, no individual can exercise authority that does not proceed from it in plain terms.

4. Liberty consists in the power to do anything that does not injure others; accordingly, the exercise of the natural rights of each man has no limits except . . . limits . . . determined only by law.

5. The law has the right to forbid only such actions as are injurious to society.

6. Law is the expression of the general will. All citizens have the right to take part personally, or by their representatives, in its formation. It must be the same for all whether it protects or punishes.

7. No man can be accused, arrested, or detained, except in the cases determined by the law and according to the forms that it has prescribed.

8. The law ought to establish only penalties that are strictly and obviously necessary, and no one can be punished except in virtue of a law established and promulgated prior to the offence and legally applied.

9. Every man being presumed innocent until he has been pronounced guilty. . . .

10. No one should be disturbed on account of his opinions, even religious, provided their manifestation does not derange the public order established by law.

11. . . . every citizen then can freely speak, write and print, subject to responsibility for the abuse of this freedom in the cases determined by law.

12. The guarantee of the rights of man and citizen requires a public force; this force then is instituted for the advantage of all and not for the personal benefit of those to whom it is entrusted.

13. For the maintenance of the public force and for the expenses of administration a general tax is indispensable; it ought to be equally apportioned among all the citizens according to their means.

14. All the citizens have the right to ascertain by themselves or by their representatives, the necessity of the public tax, to consent to it freely, to follow the employment of it. . . .

15. Society has the right to call for an account of his administration from every public agent.

16. Any society in which the guarantee of rights is not secured, or the separation of powers not determined, has no constitution at all.

17. Property being a sacred and inviolable right, no one can be deprived of it. . . .

6. Bill of Rights, United States—1791

Although the American Revolution had preceded the French by fourteen years, it was not until 1787 that the present constitution was written. Inasmuch as the leaders at the constitutional Convention tended to be conservative, it did not contain any provisions for individual rights. The liberals in adopting the new constitution insisted on the addition of a Bill of Rights. The following ten amendments were adopted in 1791.

Amendment I

Congress shall make no law respecting an establishment of religion, or prohibiting the free exercise thereof; or abridging the freedom of speech, or of the press; or the right of the people peaceably to assemble, and to petition the government for a redress of grievances.

Amendment II

A well regulated militia, being necessary to the security of a free State, the right of the people to keep and bear arms shall not be infringed.

Amendment III

No soldier shall, in time of peace, be quartered in any house, without the consent of the owner, nor in time of war, but in a manner to be prescribed by law.

Amendment IV

The right of the people to be secure in their persons, houses, papers, and effects, against unreasonable searches and seizures, shall not be violated. . . .

Amendment V

No person shall be held to answer for a capital or otherwise infamous crime . . . nor shall any person be subject for the same offence to be twice put in jeopardy of life or limb; nor shall be compelled in any criminal case to be a witness against himself, nor be deprived of life, liberty, or property, without due process of law; nor shall private property be taken for public use, without just compensation.

Amendment VI

In all criminal prosecutions the accused shall enjoy the right to a speedy and public trial, by an impartial jury of the State and district wherein the crime shall have been committed . . . and to be informed of the nature and cause of the accusation; to be confronted with the witnesses against him; to have compulsory process for obtaining witnesses in his favor, and to have the assistance of counsel for his defense.

Amendment VII

In suits at common law, where the value in controversy shall exceed twenty dollars, the right of trial by jury shall be preserved, and no fact tried by a jury shall be otherwise re-examined in any court of the United States than according to the rules of the common law.

Amendment VIII

Excessive bail shall not be required, nor excessive fines imposed, nor cruel and unusual punishments inflicted.

Amendment IX

The enumeration in the Constitution of certain rights shall not be construed to deny or disparge others retained by the people.

Amendment X

The powers not delegated to the United States by the Constitution, nor prohibited by it to the States, are reserved to the States respectively, or to the people.

C. SOCIETY

7. A Young Lady of Fashion's Day—1712

This selection covers twenty-four hours in the life of a member of the English aristocracy. How would her routine compare with a member of the middle-class or the laboring classes? Also, how would her activities compare with members of the aristocracy in other lands?

Tuesday *night.* Could not go to sleep til one in the morning for thinking of my journal.

Wednesday. *From eight till ten.* Drank two dishes of chocolate in bed, and fell asleep after them.

From ten to eleven. Eat a slice of bread and butter, drank a dish of bohea [a tea] and read *The Spectator.*

From eleven to one. At my toilette, tried a new head [dress]. Gave orders for [my lap dog] Veny to be combed and washed. [I must re-] Mem [ber]. I look best in blue.

From one till half an hour after two. Drove to the Change. Cheapened a couple of fans.

Till four. At dinner. Mem. Mr. Froth passed by in his new liveries.

From four to six. Dressed, paid a visit to old Lady Blithe and her sister, having before heard they were gone out of town that day.

From six to eleven. At basset [a game of cards]. Mem. Never set again upon the ace of diamonds.

Thursday. *From eleven at night to eight in the morning.* Dreamed that I . . . [gambled with] Mr. Froth.

8. Court Life at Versailles, Saint-Simon

Saint-Simon, the author of this selection, was a member of the French nobility who lived at Versailles during the reign of Louis XIV (1643-1715). Judging from his writings did Saint-Simon approve or disapprove of the king and court's conduct? Since Saint-Simon was a noble, how did this influence his viewpoint?

The Court was another phase of the king's domineering policy. Many things contributed to remove the residence of the Court from Paris and establish it permanently in the country. The troubles of his minority . . . had impressed him with a great aversion to it and a conviction that his stay there was dangerous; also that the residence of the Court elsewhere would make cabals with Paris less easy, although the distance might not be great, and more difficult to conceal because absences would readily be noticed.

The frequent fetes, the drives to Versailles, and the various trips elsewhere were means which the king employed to distinguish, or mortify, the persons who were or were not invited to join them, and thus to keep every one attentive and assiduous to please him. He felt that he had not enough real favours to shed around him continually; he therefore substituted ideal ones, little preferences which were shown daily, one might say momentarily, with an art that was all his own. The hopes that these small preferences and distinctions excited the consequence that people derived from them, were amazing, and no one was ever more ingenious than he in contriving such occasions. [the Palace of] Marly, in the end, was of great use to him in this respect, and also [the Palace of] Trianon where every one, it is true, might go and pay their court to him, but where, alone, ladies had the honour of eating with him and were chosen specially for each meal. There was also the honour of the candlestick to be held at his *courcher* by a courtier whom he wished to distinguish and named aloud after he had finished saying his prayers. The *justaucorps a brevet* was another of these inventions. It was blue, lined with red, the facings and waistcoat also red, embroidered magnificently in a gold design touched up with silver in a style reserved for these garments. Only a certain number of them existed; of which the king, his family, and the princes of the blood had each one, but the latter, like the rest of the courtiers, only had them when a vacancy occurred. The most distinguished personages at Court asked for them, either for themselves or for others, and it was thought a great favour to obtain them. The king invented them for those persons, very few in number, who had the privilege of accompanying him in his walks at Saint-Germain and at Versailles witut being invited; and after the walks ceased, the coats ceased to give any privilege, except that they might be worn when there was court or family mourning. The different ingenuities of this nature which succeeded each other as the king advanced in years, and fetes increased or diminished, and the attention he gave to keeping a numerous Court about him, would be endless to relate.

Not only was he desirous of the continual presence of distinguished persons, but he was just an anxious for that of the inferior ranks. He looked about him to right and left at his *lever,* his *coucher,* at his meals, as he passed through the apartments, and in his gardens at Versailles, where alone the courtiers had the liberty of following him. He saw and noticed every one; no one escaped his eye, not even those who scarcely hoped to be seen. He noted in his own mind the absence of such as were usually present, also that of occasional persons who came more or less often; he informed himself as to the causes, general or special, of such absences, and never lost the slightest occasion to act towards the persons in consequence. In his eyes it was a great demerit in the most distinguished personages if they did not make the Court their abode; it was another in those who came seldom; and it was certain disgrace to those who never, or almost never, came at all. When some favour was asked for one of the latter, "I don't know him," he would reply, haughtily. About those who came seldom, he would say, "That is a man I never see;" and the decision against such persons was irrevocable. It was another crime not to go to Fontainebleau, which he regarded as a second Versailles; and for certain persons not "to ask for Marly," some always, others often, it needed a valid excuse to save them, men and women both, from disgrace. Above all, he could not endure that persons should go to Paris and amuse themselves. He was rather easy with those who liked to go to their country-seats, but they had to be careful not to stay too long, or else have taken precautions to give notice of it.

9. Napoleon's Wardrobe for 1811-12

This wardrobe list was drawn up by Napoleon to meet his clothing needs for a year. Remembering that Napoleon prided himself on being "a child of the Revolution," what does this selection tell us about Napoleon, the man and the ruler? How would he compare with previous rulers of France?

Uniforms and Greatcoats	*Francs*
1 grenadier's tail-coat on 1st January with epaulettes, etc.	
1 chasseur's tail-coat on 1st April with epaulettes, etc.	at 360
1 grenadier's tail-coat on 1st July, with epaulettes, etc.	each =
1 chasseur's tail-coat on 17th October, with epaulettes, etc.	1,440
(Each tail-coat will have to last 3 years)	
2 hunting-coats; one for riding, in the Saint-Hubert style, the other for shooting, on 1st August	860
(These coats will have to last 3 years)	
1 civilian coat on 1st November (to last 3 years)	200
2 frock-coats: one grey, and the other another colour	400
(They will be supplied on 1st October every year, and will have to last 3 years)	

Waistcoats and Breeches

    48 pairs of breeches and white waistcoats at 80 francs   3,840

    (They are to be supplied every week, and must last 3 years)

Dressing Gowns, Pantaloons, and Vests

    2 dressing-gowns, one quilted, on 1st May, and one of
swansdown, on 1st October   500

    2 pairs of pantaloons, one quilted and one of wool,
supplied in the same way   60

    (The dressing-gowns and pantaloons will have to last 3 years)

    48 flannel vests (one a week) at 30 francs   1,440

    (The vests will have to last 3 years)

Body-linen

    4 dozen shirts (a dozen a week)   2,880

    4 dozen handerkerchiefs (a dozen a week)   576

    2 dozen cravats (one a fortnight)   720

    1 dozen black collars (one a month) which must last a year   96

    2 dozen towels (a dozen a fortnight)   200

    6 Madras night-caps (one every two months) to last 3 years   144

    2 dozen pairs of silk stockings at 18 francs (one pair a fortnight)   432

    2 dozen pairs of socks (one pair a fortnight)   432

    (All this linen, except the black collars and the night-caps,
will have to last 6 years)

Footwear

    24 pairs of shoes (one pair a fortnight, which must last two years) . . .   312

    6 pairs of boots, to last 2 years   600

Headwear

    4 hats a year, supplied with the tail-coats . . . .

Miscellaneous

    Scents, slimming mixture, eau de cologne, etc. . . . .

    Washing the linen and silk stockings . . . .

    Various expenses. Nothing to be spent without His Majesty's approval . .

        Total . . . .

D. ECONOMICS

10. English Tradesman, Defoe

Defoe was a great writer of fiction and nonfiction alike. In this brief piece, he writes sensitively about English Trade as a socioeconomic prime mover: moving Englishmen to wealth in economic status and social stature. Moreover, he quickly captures and greatly lauds English merchant capitalism.

The instances which we have given in the last chapter, abundantly make for the honour of the British traders; and . . . are very far from doing dishonour to the nobility who have from time to time entered into alliance with them; for it is very well known, that besides the benefit which we reap by being a trading nation, which is our principal glory, trade is a very different thing in England than it is in many other countries, and is carried on by persons who, both in their education and descent, are far from being the dregs of the people.

King Charles II, who was perhaps the prince of all the kings that ever reigned in England, who best understood the country and the people he governed, used to say, that the tradesmen were the only gentry in England. I make no scruple to advance these three points in honour of our country—

1. That we are the greatest trading country in the world, because we have the greatest exportation of the growth and product of our land, and of the manufacture and labour of our people; and the greatest importation and consumption of the growth, product, and manufactures of other countries from abroad, of any nation in the world.

2. That our climate is the best and most agreeable to live in, because a man can be more out of doors in England than in other countries.

3. That our men are the stoutest and best, because, strip them naked from the waist upwards, and give them no weapons at all but their hands and heels, and turn them into a room or stage, and lock them in with the like number of other men of any nation, man for man, and they shall beat the best men you shall find in the world.

As so many of our noble and wealthy families, as we have shown, are raised by and derived from trade, so it is true, and indeed it cannot well be otherwise, that many of the younger branches of our gentry, and even of the nobility itself, have descended again into the spring from whence they flowed, and have become tradesmen; and thence it is that, as I said above, our tradesmen in England are not, as it generally is in other countries, always of the meanest of our people. Nor is trade itself in England, as it generally is in other countries, the meanest thing the men can turn their hand to; but on the contrary, trade is the readiest way for men to raise their fortunes and families; and therefore it is a field for men of figure and of good families to enter upon.

Having thus done a particular piece of justice to ourselves, in the value we put upon trade and tradesmen in England, it reflects very much upon the understanding of those refined heads who pretend to depreciate that part of the nation which is so infinitely superior in wealth to the families who call themselves gentry, and so infinitely more numerous.

As to the wealth of the nation, that undoubtedly lies chiefly among the trading part of the people; and though there are a great many families raised within few years, in the late war, by great employments and by great actions abroad, to the honour of the English gentry, yet how many more families among the tradesmen have been raised to immense estates, even during the same time, by the attending circumstances by the war. And by whom have the prodigious taxes been paid, the loans supplied, and many advanced upon all occasions? By whom are the banks and companies carried on, and on whom are the customs and excises levied? Have not the trade and tradesmen borne the burden of the war? And do they not still pay four millions a year interest for the public debts? On whom are the funds levied, and by whom the public credit supported? Is not trade the inexhausted fund of all funds, and upon which all the rest depend?

As is the trade, so in proportion are the tradesmen; and how wealthy are tradesmen in almost all the several parts of England, as well as in London? How common is it to see a tradesman go off the stage, even but from mere shopkeeping, with from ten to forty thousand pounds' estate to divide among his family! When, on the contrary, take the gentry in England, from one end to the other, except a few here and there, what with excessive high living, which is of late grown so much into a disease, and the other ordinary circumstances of families, we find few families of the lower gentry, but they are in debt, and in necessitous circumstances, and a great many of greater estates also.

On the other hand, let any one who is acquainted with England, look but abroad into the several counties, especially near London, or within fifty miles of it; how are the ancient families worn out by time and family misfortunes, and the estates possessed by a new race of tradesmen, grown up into families of gentry, and established by the immense wealth gained, as I may say, behind the counter; that is, in the shop, the warehouse, and the counting-house.

How many noble seats, superior to the palaces of sovereign princes, in some countries, do we see erected within few miles of this city by tradesmen, or the sons of tradesmen, while the seats and castles of the ancient gentry, like their families, look worn out and fallen into decay!

Again; in how superior a port do our tradesmen live, to what the middling gentry either do or can support! An ordinary tradesman now, not in the city only, but in the country, shall spend more money by the year, than a gentleman of four or five hundred pounds a year too; whereas the gentleman shall at the best stand stock still just where he began, nay, perhaps, decline: and as for the lower gentry, though they are often as proud and high in their appearance as the other; as to them, I say, a shoemaker in London shall keep a better house, spend more money, clothe his family better, and yet grow rich too. It is evident where the difference lies; and estate's a pond, but trade's a spring . . . it is no wonder what the tradesmen in England fills the lists of our nobility and gentry; no wonder that the gentlemen of the best families marry tradesmen's daughters, and put their younger sons apprentices to tradesmen; and how often do these younger sons come to buy the elder sons' estates, and restore the family, when the elder and head of the house, proving rakish and extravagant, has wasted his patrimony, and is obliged to make out the blessing of Israel's family, where the younger son brought the birthright, and the elder was doomed to serve him!

Trade is so far here from being inconsistent with a gentleman, that, in short, trade in England makes gentlemen. Nor do we find any defect either in the genious or capacities of the posterity of tradesmen, arising from any remains of mechanic blood, which, it is pretended, should influence them; but all the gallantry of spirit, greatness of soul, and all the generous principles that can be found in any of the ancient families, whose blood is the most untainted, as they call it, with the low mixtures of a mechanic race, are found in these; and, as is said before, they generally go beyond them in knowledge of the world, which is the best education.

We see the tradesmen of England, as they grow wealthy, coming every day to the herald's office to search for the coats of arms of their ancestors, in order to paint them upon their coaches, and grave them upon their plate, embroider them upon their furniture, or carve them upon the pediments of their new houses; and how often do we see them trace the registers of their families up to the prime nobility, or the most ancient gentry of the kingdom!

In this search we find them often qualified to raise new families, if they do not descend from old; as was said of a certain tradesman of London, that if he could not find the ancient race of gentlemen, from which he came, he would begin a new race, who should be as good gentlemen as any that went before him.

All this confirms what I have said before, viz., that trade in England neither is or ought to be compared with what it is in other countries; or the tradesman depreciated as they are abroad, and as some of our gentry would pretend to do in England; but that as many of our best families rose from trade, so many branches of the best families in England, under the nobility, have stooped so low as to be put apprentices to tradesmen in London, and to set up and follow those trades when they have come out of their times, and have thought it no dishonour to their blood.

11. Economic Liberty, Adam Smith

Adam Smith was and is the most famous Western economist. And he founded the classic school of economic liberalism. In this quaint and curious selection, he formulates his famous English economic thesis: although ironically it later is to be given a French title: laissez-faireism, with emphasis upon individual efforts whether this individualism be within a specific family, a particular business, or a nation large or small. Then religiously, his warning is that there must be separation of economics from politics.

As every individual, therefore, endeavours as much as he can both to employ his capital in the support of domestic industry, and so to direct that industry that its produce may be of the greatest value; every individual necessarily labours to render the annual revenue of the society as great as he can. He generally, indeed, neither intends to promote the public interest, nor knows how much he is promoting it. By preferring the support of domestic to that of foreign industry, he intends only his own security; and by directing that industry in such a manner as its produce may be of the greatest value, he intends only his own gain, and he is in this, as in many other cases, led by an invisible hand to promote an end which was no part of his intention. Nor is it always the worse for the society that it was no part of it. By pursuing his own interest he frequently promotes that of the society more effectually than when he really intends to promote it. I have never known much good done by those who affected to trade for the public good. It is an affectation, indeed, not very common among merchants, and very few words need be employed in dissuading them from it.

What is the species of domestic industry

which his capital can employ, and of which the produce is likely to be of the greatest value, every individual, it is evident, can, in his local situation, judge much better than any statesman or lawgiver can do for him. The statesman, who should attempt to direct private people in what manner they ought to employ their capitals, would not only load himself with a most unnecessary attention, but assume an authority which culd safely be trusted, not only to no single person, but to no council or senate whatever, and which would nowhere be so dangerous as in the hands of a man who had folly and presumption enough to fancy himself fit to exercise it.

To give the monopoly of the home market to the produce of domestic industry, in any particular art or manufacture, is in some measure to direct private people in what manner they ought to employ their capitals, and must, in almost all cases, be either a useless or a hurtful regulation. If the produce of domestic can be brought these as cheap as that of foreign industry, the regulation is evidently useless. If it cannot, it must generally be hurtful. It is the maxim of every prudent master of a family, never to attempt to make at home what it will cost him more to make than to buy. The taylor does not attempt to make his own shoes, but buys them of the shoemaker. The shoemaker does not attempt to make his own clothes, but employes a taylor. The farmer attempts to make neither the one nor the other, but employs those different artificers. All of them find it for their interest to employ their whole industry in a way in which they have some advantage over their neighbours, and to purchase with a part of its produce, or what is the same thing, with the price of a part of it, whatever else they have occasion for.

What is prudence in the conduct of every private family, can scarce be folly in that of a great kingdom. If a foreign country can supply us with a commodity cheaper than we ourselves can make it, better buy it of them with some part of the produce of our own industry, employed in a way in which we have some advantage. The general industry of the country, being always in proportion to the capital which employs it, will not thereby be diminished, no more than that of the above-mentioned artificers; but only left to find out the way in which it can be employed with the greatest advantage. It is certainly not employed to the greatest advantage, when it is thus directed towards an object which it can buy cheaper than it can make. The value of its annual produce is certainly more or less diminished, when it is thus turned away from producing commodities evidently of more value than the commodity which it is directed to produce. According to the supposition, that commodity could be purchased from foreign countries cheaper than it can be made at home. It could, therefore, have been purchased with a part only of the commodities, or, what is the same thing, with a part only of the price of the commodities, which the industry employed by an egual capital would have produced at home, had it been left to follow its natural course. The industry of the country, therefore, is thus turned away from a more, to a less advantageous employment, and the exchangeable value of its annual produce, instead of being increased, according to the intention of the lawgiver, must necessarily be diminished by every such regulation.

12. **English Commerce, Voltaire**

Voltaire was in all likelihood the first world-famous writer. His French observations on

English commerce do not reflect his literary facility and felicity at their best; but his economic insights about England from an outsider-French perspective may add respect for economic growth, and as an additional dividend respect for the universal viewpoint of Voltaire himself.

Carthage, Venice, and Amsterdam were undoubtedly powerful; but their conduct has been exactly like that of merchants grown rich by traffic, who afterwards purchase lands that carry with them the dignity of lordship. Neither Carthage, Venice, nor Holland have, from a warlike and even conquering beginning, ended in a commercial nation. The English are the only people in existence who have done this; they were for a long time warriors before they learned to cast accounts. They were entirely ignorant of numbers when they won the battles of Agincourt, Crecy, and Poitiers, and were also ignorant that it was in their power to become corn merchants and woollen drapers, two things that would certainly turn to much better account than winning battles. This science alone has rendered the nation at once populous, wealthy, and powerful. London was a poor country town when Edward III conquered one half of France; and it is wholly owing to this that the English have become merchants; that London exceeds Paris in extent and number of inhabitants; that they are able to equip and man two hundred said of ships of war, and keep the things who are their allies in pay. The Scots are born warriors, and, from the purity of their air, inherit good sense. Whence comes it then that Scotland, under the name of a Union, has become a province of England? It is because Scotland has scarcely any other commodity than coal, and that England has fine tin, excellent wood, and abounds in corn, manufactures, and trading companies.

Even the younger son of a peer of the realm is not above trading. Lord Townshend, secretary of state, has a brother who is satisfied with being a merchant in the city.

At the time when Lord Oxford ruled all England, his younger brother was a trader at Aleppo, whence he could never be prevailed on to return, and where he died. This custom which is now unhappily dying out, appears monstrous to a German, whose head is full of the coats of arms and the pageant of his family. They can never conceive how it is possible that the son of an English peer should be no more than a rich and powerful citizen, when in Germany they are all princes. I have known more than thirty highnesses of the same name, whose whole fortune and estate put together amounted to a few coats of arms, and the starving pride they inherited from their ancestors.

In France everybody is a marquis; and a man just come from the obscurity of some remote province, with money in his pocket and a name that ends in *"ac"* or *"ille,"* may give himself airs, and usurp such phrases as "A man of my quality and rank"; and hold merchants in the most sovereign contempt. The merchant again, by dint of hearing his profession despised on all occasions, at last is fool enough to blush at his condition. I will not, however, take it upon me to say which is the most useful to his country, and which of the two ought to have the pre ference; whether the powdered lord, who knows to a minute when the king rises or goes to bed, perhaps to stool, and who gives himself airs of importance while playing the part of a slave in the antechamber of a minister; or the merchant, who enriches his country, and from his counting house sends his orders into Surat or Cairo, thereby contributing to the happiness and convenience of human nature.

13. State of English Agriculture in 1770

This is a good triple economic statement, for it shows: (1) that English husbandry "wanted improvement," (2) that there were sophisticated English economic observers such as Arthur Young, and (3) even the English agricultural revolution (to say nothing of the industrial revolution) was tortuously slow in growth and development.

. . . his Lordship [the Marquis of Rockingham] found the husbandry of the West Riding of Yorkshire extremely deficient in numerous particulars. It was disgusting to him to view so vast a property cultivated in so slovenly a manner; eager to substitute better methods in the room of such unpleasing as well as unprofitable ones, he determined to exert himself with spirit in the attempt; and he executed the noble scheme in a manner that does honor to his penetration. A very few particulars, among many of the common practice, will show how much this country wanted a Rockingham to animate its cultivation.

1. Large tracts of land, both grass and arable, yielded but a trifling profit, for want of draining. In wet clays, the rushes and other aquatic rubbish usurped the place of corn and grass; the seasons of tilling were retarded, and even destroyed, and those pastures which ought to have fed an ox, scarcely maintained a sheep.

2. The pastures and meadows of this country were universally laid down in ridge and furrow, a practice highly destructive of profit, and detestable to the eye; and the manner of laying down such lands was as miserable as their product denoted poverty; for after many years ploughing of numerous crops but insufficient fallows, when the soil was so exhausted as to disappoint the expection of corn, a parcel of rubbish called hayseeds was scattered over the surface, and the field left to time for improvement. A villainous custom, and too much practiced in all parts of the kingdom.

3. The culture of turnips was become common, but in such a method that their introduction was undoubtedly a real mischief; *viz.*, without hoeing, so that the year of fallow, in the general management, was the most capital year of slovenliness and bad husbandry.

4. The implements used in agriculture through this tract were insufficient for a vigorous culture, and consequently the husbandman sustained a constant loss.

These circumstances, among others, show how much the husbandry of this country wanted improvement. . . .

E. SOURCES FOR PART IV

1. Baruch Spinoza, *Tractatus Theologico-Politicus,* trans. by R.H.M. Elwes, 2nd ed.; London: George Bill & Sons, 1899.
2. John Morley (ed.), *The Works of Voltaire,* Paris: Dumont, 1901.
3. Benjamin Franklin, *The Autobiography,* from *The Complete Works,* ed. by John Bigelow; New York: G.P. Putnam's Sons, 1887. Vol. II.
4. James H. Robinson (ed.), *Op. Cit.*
5. F.M. Anderson, *Constitutions and Other Select Documents Illustrative of the History of France,* Minneapolis: 1908.
6. United States Constitution, Articles I thru X.
7. Joseph Addison (ed.) *The Spectator* (March 11, 1712).
8. Duc de Saint-Simon, *Memoirs,* trans. by K.P. Wormeley, Boston: 1899.

9. *Correspondence de Napoleon, vol. xxii;* Paris: n.d.
10. Daniel Defoe, *The Complete English Tradesman,* London: 1724.
11. Adam Smith, *An Inquiry into the Nature and Causes of the Wealth of Nations,* London: 1802.
12. Morley, *The Works of Voltaire.*
13. Arthur Young, *A Six Months Tour Through the North of England,* London: 1770.

V
MODERN CIVILIZATION

A. ETHICS

1. Darwinism, Wallace

Alfred Wallace (1823-1913) was an English natural scientist who worked out a theory of evolution independently of Charles Darwin. The theory of evolution shook almost every religious ethic by attacking revelation including Divine creation as set forth in the Bible.

The Change of Opinion Effected by Darwin

The point I wish especially to urge is this. Before Darwin's work appeared, the great majority of naturalists, and almost without exception the whole literary and scientific world, held firmly to the belief that species were realities, and had not been derived from other species by any process accessible to us. . . . But now this is all changed. The whole scientific and literary world, even the whole educated public, accepts, as a matter of common knowledge, the origin of species from other allied species by the ordinary process of natural birth. The idea of special creation or any altogether exceptional mode of production is absolutely extinct! Yet more: this is held also to apply to many higher groups as well as to the species of a genus, and not even Mr. Darwin's severest critics venture to suggest that the primeval bird, reptile, or fish must have been "specially created." And this vast, this totally unprecedented change in public opinion has been the result of the work of one man, and was brought about in the short space of twenty years! This is the answer to those who continue to maintain that the "origin of species" is not yet discovered; that there are still doubts and difficulties; that there are divergencies of structure so great that we cannot understand how they had their beginning. We may admit all this. . . . But we claim for Darwin that he is the Newton of natural history, and that, just so surely as that the discovery and demonstration by Newton of the law of gravitation established order in place of chaos and laid a sure foundation for all future study of the starry heavens, so surely has Darwin, by his discovery of the law of natural selection and his demonstration of the great principle of the preservation of useful variations in the struggle for life, not only thrown a flood of light on the process of development of the whole organic world, but also established a firm foundation for all future study of nature.

In order to show the view Darwin took of his own work, and what it was that he alone claimed to have done, the concluding passage of the introduction to the *Origin of Species* should be carefully considered. It is as follows: "Although much remains obscure, and will long remain obscure, I can entertain no doubt, after the most deliberate and dispassionate judgment of which I am capable, that the view which most naturalists until recently entertained and which I formerly entertained—namely, that each species has been independently created—is erroneous. I am fully convinced that species are not immutable; but that those belonging to what are called the same genera are lineal descendants of some other and generally extinct species, in the same manner as the acknowledged varieties of any one species are the descendants of that species. Furthermore, I am convinced that Natural Selection has been the most important, but not the exclusive, means of modification."

The Darwinian Theory

The theory of natural selection rests on two main classes of facts which apply to all organized beings without exception, and which thus take rank as fundamental principles or laws. The first is, the power of rapid multiplication in a geometrical progression; the second, that the offspring always vary slightly from the parents, though generally very loosely resembling them. From the first fact or law there follows, necessarily, a constant struggle for existence; because, while the offspring always exceed the parents in number, generally to an enormous extent, yet the total number of living organisms in the world does not, and cannot, increase year by year. Consequently every year, on the average, as many die as are born, plants as well as animals; and the majority die premature deaths.

Then comes the question, Why do some live rather than others? If all the individuals of each species were exactly alike in every respect, we could only say it is a matter of chance. But they are not alike. We find that they vary in many different ways. We cannot doubt that, on the whole, any beneficial variations will give the possessors of it a greater probability of living through the tremendous ordeal they have to undergo. There may be something left to chance, but on the whole the fittest will survive.

The Ethical Aspect of the Struggle for Existence

Our exposition of the phenomena presented by the struggle for existence may be fitly concluded by a few remarks on its ethical aspect. Now that the war of nature is better known, it has been dwelt upon by many writers as presenting so vast an amount of cruelty and pain as to be revolting to our instincts of humanity, while it has proved a stumbling-block in the way of those who would fain believe in an all-wise and benevolent ruler of the universe.

Now there is, I think, good reason to believe that all this is greatly exaggerated; that the supposed "torments" and "miseries" of animals have little real existence, but are the reflection of the imagined sensations of cultivated men and women in similar circumstances; and that the amount of actual suffering caused by the struggle for existence among animals is altogether insignificant. . . .

Thus the poet's picture of "Nature red in tooth and claw with ravine" is a picture the evil of which is read into it by our imaginations, the reality being made up of full and happy lives, usually terminated by the quickest and least painful of deaths.

On the whole, then, we conclude that the popular idea of the struggle for existence entailing misery and pain on the animal world is the very reverse of the truth. What it really brings about, is, the maximum of life and of the enjoyment of life with the minimum of suffering and pain. Given the necessity of death and reproduction—and without these there could have been no progressive development of the organic world,—and it is difficult then to imagine a system by which a greater balance of happiness could have been secured. And this view was evidently that of Darwin himself, who thus concludes his chapter on the struggle for existence: "When we reflect on this struggle, we may console ourselves with the full belief that the war of nature is not incessant, that no fear is felt, that death is generally prompt, and that the vigorous, the healthy, and the happy survive and multiply."

2. Ethics, Huxley

Thomas Huxley (1825-95) was an English biologist who was also a leading advocate of Darwinism. In this selection Huxley explores the relationship between evolution and ethics.

As no man fording a swift stream can dip his foot twice into the same water, so no man can, with exactness, affirm of anything in the sensible world that it is. As he utters the words, nay, as he thinks them, the predicate ceases to be applicable; the present has become the past; the "is" should be "was." And the more we learn of the nature of things, the more evident is it that what we call rest is only unperceived activity; that seeming peace is silent but strenuous battle. In every part, at every moment, the state of the cosmos is the expression of a transitory adjustment of contending forces. . . . Thus the most obvious attribute of the cosmos is its impermanence. It assumes the aspect not so much of a permanent entity as of a changeful process, in which naught endures save the flow of energy and the national order which pervades it.

We are more than sufficiently familiar with modern pessimism. . . . We also know modern speculative optimism, with its perfectibility of the species, reign of peace, and lion and lamb transformation scenes; but one does not hear so much of it as one did forty years ago. . . . The majority of us . . . profess neither pessimism nor optimism. We hold that the world is neither so good, nor so bad, as it conceivably might be. . . .

Further, I think I do not err in assuming that, however, diverse their views on philosophical and religious matters, most men are agreed that the proportion of good and evil in life may be very sensibly affected by human action. . . . Nobody professes to doubt that, so far forth as we possess a power of bettering things, it is our paramount duty to use it and to train all our intellect and energy to this supreme service of our kind.

Hence the pressing interest of the question, to what extent modern progress in natural knowledge, and, more especially, the general outcome of that progress in the doctrine of evolution, is competent to help us in the great work of helping one another?

The propounders of what are called the "ethics of evolution," when the "evolution of ethics" would usually better express the object of their speculations, adduce a number of more or less interesting facts and more or less sound arguments, in favour of the origin of the moral sentiments, in the same way as other natural phenomena, by a process of evolution . . . but as the immoral sentiments have no less been evolved, there is, so far, as much natural sanction for the one as the other. The thief and the murderer follow nature just as much as the philanthropist.

There is another fallacy which appears to me to pervade the so-called "ethics of evolution." It is the notion that because, on the whole, animals and plants have advanced in perfection of organization by means of the struggle for existence and the consequent "survival of the fittest"; therefore men in society, men as ethical beings, must look to the same process to help them towards perfection. I suspect that this fallacy has arisen out of the unfortunate ambiguity of the phrase "survival of the fittest." "Fittest" has a connotation of "best"; and about "best" there hangs a moral flavour. In cosmic nature, however, what is "fittest" depends upon the conditions.

Men in society are undoubtedly subject to the cosmic process. As among other animals, multiplication goes on without cessation, and involves severe competition for the means of support. The struggle for existence tends to eliminate those less fitted to adapt themselves to the circumstances of their existence. But the influence of the cosmic processes on the evolution of society is the greater the more rudimentary its civilization. Social progress means a checking of the cosmic process at every step and the substitution for it of another, which may be called the ethical process; the end of which is not the survival of those who may happen to be the fittest, in respect of the whole of the conditions which obtain, but of those who are ethically the best.

As I have already urged, the practice of that which is ethically best—what we call goodness or virtue—involves a course of conduct which, in all respects, is opposed to that which leads to success in the cosmic struggle for existence. In place of ruthless self-assertion it demands self-restraint; in place of thrusting aside, or treading down, all competitors, it requires that the individual shall not merely respect, but shall help his fellows; its influence is directed, not so much to the survival of the fittest, as to the fitting of as many as possible to survive. Laws and moral precepts are directed to the end of curbing the cosmic process and reminding the individual of his duty to the community, to the protection and influence of which he owes, if not existence itself, at least the life of something better than a brutal savage.

Let us understand, once for all, that the ethical progress of society depends, not on imitating the cosmic process, still less in running away from it, but in combating it.

Ethical nature may count upon having to reckon with a tenacious and powerful enemy as long as the world lasts. And much may be done to change the nature of man himself. The intelligence which has converted the brother of the wolf into the faithful guardian of the flock ought to be able to do something towards curbing the instincts of savagery in civilized men.

3. Beyond Good and Evil, Nietzsche

Friedrich Nietzsche (1844-1900) was a brilliant but unstable German philosopher whose writings were critical of Christian ethics as a "slave morality" and include the concept of the "superman" who reflects the "will to power" and conforms to a "master morality." The reader may wish to speculate on the influence of Nietzsche upon selection one in part VI.

Life as Exploitation

Life itself is *essentially* appropriating, injuring and vanquishing of what is foreign and weak: it is suppression, severity, obtrusion of its own forms, incorporation and, at least putting it most milding, exploitation; but why should one forever use precisely these words on which for ages a disreputable significance has been stamped? Even an organization within which individuals deal with one another on equal terms (it is so in every healthy aristocracy) must, if it is a living and not a dying organization, act hostilely towards other organizations in all matters wherein the several individuals restrain themselves in their dealings with one another; it must be the embodied Will to Power, it has to seek to grow, it has to endeavor to gain ground, obtain advantage and acquire ascendancy—not on account of any morality or immorality whatsoever, but because it *lives,* and because life itself *is* Will to Power.

There is nothing, however, on which the ordinary consciousness of Europeans is more unwilling to be corrected than on this matter; at present people rave everywhere . . . about coming conditions of society in which "the exploiting character" will be absent: that sounds to me as if they proposed to invent a mode of life which should not exercise organic functions. "Exploitation" does not belong to a depraved or an imperfect and primitive state of society; it belongs to the essence of living beings . . . it is a consequence of the intrinsic Will to Power, which is just the Will to Life. Granting that as a theory this is an innovation, as a reality it is the original fact of history.

Master-Morality and Slave-Morality

In strolling through the many finer and coarser forms of morality which have hitherto prevailed or yet prevail on the earth, I found certain characteristics recurring regularly in connection with one another, until at last two fundamental types betrayed themselves to me, and a fundamental distinction was brought to light. There is *Master-morality and Slave-morality.* . . . The distinctions of moral worth have arisen either in a ruling caste, agreeably conscious of being distinct from the ruled; or among the ruled themselves. In the first case, when it is the ruling caste that determines the conception "good," it is the exalted, proud disposition which is regarded as distinguishing and decisive as to the degree of rank. The noble type of man separates from himself those in whom the opposite of this is exalted, proud disposition displays itself—he despises them. . . . The despised ones are the cowards, the timid, the insignificant, those thinking merely of narrow utility . . . and, above all, the liars— it is a fundamental belief of all aristocrats that the common people are deceitful. . . .

It is obvious that the designations of moral worth everywhere were at first applied to *men,* and were only derivatively and at a later period applied to actions. The noble type of man regards *himself* as the determiner of worth, it is not necessary for him to be approved of, he passes the judgment . . . he recognizes that it is he himself only that confers honor on things—he is *a creator of worth,* of values. The noble man honors the powerful one in himself, and also him who has self-command, who knows how to speak and keep silence, who joyfully exercises strictness and severity over himself and reverences all that is strict and severe. The noble and brave who think thus are furthest removed from the morality which sees precisely in sympathy, in acting for the good of others, or in disinterestedness, the characteristic of morality; a belief in oneself, a pride in oneself, a fundamental hostility and irony with respect to "selflessness," belong as distinctly to the higher morality as do careless scorn and precaution in presence of sympathy and the "warm heart." The profound reverence for age and tradition—all law rests on this double reverence—the belief and prejudice in favor of ancestors and unfavorable to newcomers, is typical of the morality of the powerful; and if, reversely, men of "modern ideas" believe almost instinctively in "progress" and "the future," and are more and more lacking in respect for the old, the ignoble origin of these "ideas" complacently betrays itself thereby.

The morality of the ruling class, however, is more especially foreign and irritating to the taste of the present day, owing to the sternness of the principle that one has only obligations to one's equals, that one may act towards beings of a lower rank, and towards all that is foreign to one, according to discretion, or "as the heart desires," and in any case "beyond Good and Evil."

It is different with the second type of morality, Slave-morality. The slave contemplates with disapproval the virtues of the powerful; he has a thorough skepticism and distrust, a *refinement* of distrust, of everything "good" that is there honored. . . . On the other hand, *those* qualities are brought into prominence and into the light which tends to alleviate the existence of sufferers; it is here that the kind helping hand, the warm heart, along with sympathy, patience, diligence, submissiveness and friendliness attain to honor; for these are the most useful qualities here, and almost the only expedients for supporting the burden of existence. Slave-morality is essentially the morality of utility. This is the seat of the origin of the celebrated antithesis "good" and "evil"; the notion of power and dangerousness is introduced into the evil. . . . According to slave-morality, the "evil" man also excites fear; according to master-morality, it is precisely the "good" man who excites fear and seeks to excite it, while the "bad" man is regarded as the contemptible being. The contrast attains its maximum when, according to the logical consequences involved, a tinge of depreciation attaches itself to the "good" man of slave-morality; because in any case he has to be the *safe* man. . . .

A last fundamental distinction: the desire for *liberty,* the instinct for happiness, and the refinements of the feeling of freedom, belong as necessarily to the domain of slave-morals and slave-morality; as enthusiasm and art in reverence and devotion are the regular symptoms of an aristocratic mode of thinking and valuing.

B. LAW

4. Holy Alliance—1815

The extremes of the French Revolution and the Napoleonic Wars that followed convinced European leaders of the dangers of giving rights and liberties to their subjects. The first half of the nineteenth century became one of repression. One of the first instruments was the so-called Holy Alliance, under which the rulers of Russia, Prussia, and Austria declared themselves as agents of God to justify their repressive measures.

In the Name of the very Holy and Indivisible Trinity.

Their majesties, the Emperor of Austria, the King of Prussia and the Emperor of Russia . . . having reached the profound conviction that the policy of the powers, in their mutual relations, ought to be guided by the sublime truths taught by the eternal religion of God our Saviour, solemnly declare that the present act has no other aim than to manifest to the world their unchangeable determination to adopt no other rule of conduct, either in the government of their respective countries or in their holy religion, than the precepts of justice, charity and peace. Hence their majesties have agreed upon the following articles:

Article I. Conformably to the words of Holy Scripture which command all men to look upon each other as brothers, the three contracting monarchs will continue united by the bonds of a true and indissoluble fraternity, and regarding themselves as compatriots, they will lend aid and assistance to each other on all occasions and in all places; viewing themselves, in their relations to their subjects and to their armies, as fathers of families, they will direct them in that spirit of fraternity by which they are animated, for the protection of religion, peace and justice.

Article II. Hence the sole principle of conduct, be it between the said governments or their subjects, shall be that of rendering mutual service, and testifying by unceasing goodwill, the mutual affection with which they should be animated. Considering themselves all as members of one great Christian nation, the three allied princes look upon themselves as delegates of Providence called upon to govern three branches of the same family, viz: Austria, Russia and Prussia.

They thus confess that the Christian nation, of which they and their people form a part, has in reality no other sovereign than He alone to whom belongs by right the power. . . . Their majesties recommend, therefore, to their peoples, as the sole means of enjoying that peace which springs from a good conscience and is alone enduring, to fortify themselves each day in the principles and practice of those duties which the Divine Saviour has taught to men.

Article III. All those powers who wish solemnly to make avowal of the sacred principles which have dictated the present act, and who would recognize how important it is to the happiness of nations . . . that these truths should hereafter exercise upon human destiny all the influence belonging to them, shall be received into this Holy Alliance with as much cordiality as affection.

Engrossed in three copies and signed at Paris, year of grace 1815, September 14/26

Signed: Francis
Frederick William
Alexander

5. Carlsbad Decrees—1819

The German universities and their concept of Leherfreiheit-Lernfreiheit (academic freedom), became centers of liberal thought in the German Confederation. Following a series of demonstrations against the establishment and the assassination of one of the conservative leaders, the Confederation legislature, under the leaership of Metternich, passed the Carlsbad Decrees in order to curb the intellectuals.

1. A special representative of the ruler of each state shall be appointed for each university, with appropriate instructions and extended powers, and shall reside in the place where the university is situated. . . .

The function of this agent shall be to see to the strictest enforcement of existing laws and disciplinary regulations; to observe carefully . . . the instructors in the university in their public lectures and regular courses, and, without directly interfering in scientific matters or in the methods of teaching, to give a salutary direction to the instruction. . . .

2. The confederated governments mutually pledge themselves to remove from the uni-

versities or other public education institutions all teachers who, by obvious deviation from their duty, or by exceeding the limits of their functions, or by the abuse of their legitimate influence over the youthful minds, or by propagating harmful doctrines hostile to public order or subversive of existing governmental institutions, shall have unmistakably proved their unfitness for the important office intrusted to them . . .

No teacher who shall have been removed in this manner shall be again appointed to a position in any public institution of learning in another state of the union.

3. Those laws which have for a long period been directed against secret and unauthorized societies in the universities shall be strictly enforced. These laws apply especially to that association established some years since under the name Universal Students' Union. . . . The duty of especial watchfulness in this matter should be impressed upon the special agents of the government.

The governments mutually agree that such persons as shall hereafter be shown to have remained in secret or unauthorized associations, or shall have entered such associations, shall not be admitted to any public office.

4. No student who shall be expelled from a university by a decision of the university senate which was ratified or prompted by the agent of the government, or who shall have left the institution in order to escape expulsion, shall be received in any other university. . . .

6. Revolutions of 1848, Schurz

After more than three decades of oppression, Europe exploded into a series of Revolutions in 1848. Karl Schurz mirrors the idealistic hopes of the liberals and nationalists. Incidently, he did become involved and when they failed, he joined the stream of liberal refugees to the United States, where he eventually became a U.S. Senator and cabinet member.

One morning toward the end of February 1848, I sat quietly in my attic chamber, working hard at my tragedy of *Ulrich von Hutten,* when suddenly a friend rushed breathlessly into the room, exclaiming: "What, you sitting here! Do you not know what has happened?"

"No; what?"

"The French have driven away Louis Philippe and proclaimed the republic."

I threw down my pen. . . . We tore down the stairs, into the street, to the market square, the accustomed meeting place for all the student societies after their midday dinner. Although it was still forenoon, the market was already crowded with young men talking excitedly. There was no shouting, no noise, only agitated conversation. What did we want there? This probably no one knew. But since the French had driven away Louis Philippe and proclaimed the republic, something of course must happen here, too. Some of the students had brought their rapiers along, as if it were necessary to make an attack or to defend themselves. We were dominated by a vague feeling as if a great outbreak of elemental forces had begun, as if an earthquake were impending of which we had felt the first shock, and we instinctively crowded together. Thus we wandered about in numerous bands—to the *Kneipe,* where our restlessness, however, would not suffer us long to stay; . . . we fell into conversation with all manner of strangers, to find in them the same confused, astonished, and expectant state of mind; then back to the market square, to see what might be going on there; until finally late in the night fatigue compelled us to find the way home.

The next morning there were the usual lectures to be attended. But how profitless! The voice of the professor sounded like a monotonous drone coming from far away. What he had to say did not seem to concern us. The pen that should have taken notes remained idle. At last we closed our notebooks with a sigh and went away, impelled by a feeling that now we had something more important to do—to devote ourselves to the affairs of the fatherland. And this we did by seeking again as quickly as possible the company of our friends, in order to discuss what had happened and what was to come. In these conversations, excited as they were, certain ideas and catchwords worked themselves to the surface, which expressed more or less the feelings of the people. Now had arrived in Germany the day for the establishment of "German Unity," and the founding of a great, powerful national German empire.

First in line the convocation of a national parliament. Then the demands for civil rights and liberties, free speech, free press, the right of free assembly, equality before the law, a freely elected representation of the people with legislative power, responsibility of ministers, self-government of the communes, the right of the people to carry arms, the formation of a civic guard with elective officers and so on—in short, that which was called a "Constitutional form of government of a broad democratic basis." Republican ideas were at first only sparingly expressed. But the word democracy was soon on all tongues, and many, too, thought it a matter of course that if the princes should try to withhold from the people rights and liberties demanded, force would take the place of mere petition. Of course the regeneration of the country must, if possible, be accomplished by peaceable means. A few days after the outbreak of this commotion I reached my nineteenth birthday. I remember to have been so entirely absorbed by what was happening that I could hardly turn my thoughts to anything else. Like many of my friends, I was dominated by the feeling that at last the great opportunity had arrived for giving to the German people the liberty which was their birthright and to the German fatherland its unity and greatness, and that it was now the first duty of every German to do and to sacrifice everything for this sacred object. We were profoundly, solemnly, in earnest. . . .

7. Revolutions of 1848, British Press

Continuing the previous selection, this is typical of the reports of early successes of the revolutions. Like most of the others, it would eventually be crushed.

The news of the French Revolution acted like an electric shock upon Italy. . . . The struggle commenced at Milan where, notwithstanding the old hereditary connection between that territory and the House of Austria, the feeling of hatred against the latter was most intense.

Before, however, proceeding to hostilities, the Milanese demanded: 1. The suppression of the old police, and the establishment of a new corps under the orders of the Municipality. 2. The abolition of the laws regarding state offences, and the immediate liberation of the political prisoners. 3. A provisional regency of the kingdom. 4. Liberty of the press. 5. The convocation of the district councils for the purpose of electing a National Assembly. 6. . . . A Civic Guard under the orders of the Municipality.

A crowd assembled before the Government House, and, becoming tumultuous, the soldiers on duty fired a blank volley. A boy, only sixteen years old, then drew out a pistol, and shouting *Viva l'Italia,* discharged it at the troops. The mob rushed forward and overpowered the guard; the Vice-Governor O'Donnell was made prisoner, and the tricolour flag was hoisted on the palace of the Government. This happened on the 17th of March.

On the following day . . . signals of modern insurrection were everywhere raised in the streets. . . . By . . . the 23rd . . . the Austrian troops retired in two columns on Verona and Mantua . . . At the same time the Provisional Government at Milan issued an energetic proclamation calling upon all Italians to join in the contest . . . They said:

"Fellow Citizens: We have conquered. We have compelled the enemy to fly, oppressed by his own shame as much as by our valour . . . To arns, then, to arms, to secure the fruits of our glorious revolution—to fight the last battle of independence and the Italian Union. . . ."

8. Communist Manifesto, Marx

In the midst of the Revolutions of 1848 Karl Marx issued his famous manifesto. Although it was noted by very few at the time; it was enough to have him expelled from Brussels. Up to this point it had been the emerging middle class versus the entrenched upper. Karl Marx helped the working class to see their position.

. . . The history of all hitherto existing society is the history of class struggles. Freeman and slave, patrician and plebeian, lord and serf, guild-master and journeyman—in a word, oppressor and oppressed. . . .

The modern bourgeois society, that has sprouted from the ruins of feudal society, has not done away with class antagonisms . . . Our epoch . . . simplified the class antagonisms. Society as a whole is more and more splitting up into two great hostile camps . . . Bourgeoisie and Proletariat. . . .

An oppressed class under the sway of the feudal nobility, an armed and self-governing association in the medieval commune . . . the bourgeoisie has at last, since the establishment of modern industry and of the world market, conquered for itself, in the modern representative state, exclusive political sway. . . .

The bourgeoisie . . . has pitilessly . . . left remaining no other nexus between man and man than naked self-interest, than callous "cash-payment." . . . For exploitation veiled by religious and political illusions it has substituted naked, shameless, direct brutal exploitation.

. . . The first step in the revolution by the working class, is to raise the proletariat to the position of ruling class, to win the battle of democracy. The proletariat will use its political supremacy, to wrest, by degrees, all capital from the bourgeoisie, to centralize all instruments of production in the hands of the state, . . . and to increase the total of productive forces as rapidly as possible.

9. Universal Sufferage, Bismarck

One of the leading demands of the nineteenth century liberals was for universal manhood suffrage. Surprisingly enough, it was the conservative leader Bismarck who was one of the first to give it. In this selection he gives his rationale for it. Although women were not included at this point, this minority group would gain it in the twentieth century.

Looking to the necessity, in a fight against an overwhelming foreign Power, of being able, in extreme need, to use even revolutionary means, I had had no hesitation whatever in throwing into the frying-pan, by means of the circular dispatch of June 10, 1866, the most powerful ingredient known at that time to liberty-mongers, namely, universal suffrage, so as to frighten off foreign monarchies from trying to stick a finger into our national omelette. I never doubted that the German people would be strong and clever enough to free themselves from the existing suffrage as soon as they realized that it was a harmful institution. The acceptance of universal suffrage was a weapon in the war against Austria and other foreign countries, in the war for German Unity, as well as a threat to use the last weapons in a struggle against coalitions. In a war of this sort, when it becomes a matter of life and death, one does not look at the weapons that one seizes; nor at the value of what one destroys in using them: one is guided at the moment by no other thought than the issue of the war, and the preservation of one's external independence. . . . Moreover, I still hold that the principle of universal suffrage is a just one, not only in theory but also in practice, provided always that voting be not secret, for secrecy is a quality that is indeed incompatible with the best characteristics of German blood.

The influence and the dependence on others that the practical life of man brings in its train are God-given realities which we cannot and must not ignore. If we refuse to transfer them to political life, and base that life on a faith in the secret insight of everybody, we fall into a contradiction between public law and the realities of human life which practically leads to constant frictions, and finally to an explosion, and to which there is no theoretical solution except by way of the insanities of social-democracy, the support given to which rests on the fact that the judgment of the masses is sufficiently stultified and undeveloped. . . .

The counterpoise to this lies in the influence of the educated classes which would be greatly strengthened if voting were public. . . . It may be that the greater discretion of the more intelligent classes rests on the material basis of the preservation of their possessions. The other motive, the struggle for gain, is equally justifiable; but a preponderance of those who represent property is more serviceable for the security and development of the state. A state, the control of which lies in the hands of the greedy, of the new rich, and or orators who have in a higher degree than others the capacity for deceiving the unreasoning masses, will constantly be doomed. . . . Ponderous masses, and among these the life and development of great nations must be reckoned, can only move with caution, since the road on which they travel to an unknown future has no smooth iron rails. Every great state-commonwealth that loses the prudent and restraining influence of the propertied class, whether that influence rests on material or moral grounds, will always end by being rushed along at a speed which must shatter the coach of state. . . . The element of greed has the preponderance arising from large masses which in the long run must make its way. It is in the interests of the great mass itself to wish decision to take place without dangerous acceleration of the speed of the coach of state, and without its destruction. If this should happen, however, the wheel of history will revolve again, and always in a proportionately shorter time, to dictatorship, to despotism, to absolutism, because in the end the masses yield to the need of order. . . .

C. SOCIETY

10. Conditions of the Working Class, 1820s-30s and
11. Sanitary Conditions, 1830s-40s

Great Britain was the first nation to experience the Industrial Revolution and a tremendous growth of its cities. One of the great debates among historians has been the exact nature of industrialization's impact upon the laboring classes. These two selections provide us with some insight into the quality of life in industrialized, urban Britain. How do the circumstances described in these readings compare with today?

The population employed in the cotton factories rises at five o'clock in the morning, works in the mills from six till eight o'clock, and returns home for half an hour to forty minutes to breakfast. This meal generally consists of tea or coffee with a little bread. Oatmeal porridge is sometimes, but of late rarely used, and chiefly by the men; but the stimulus of tea is preferred, and especially by the women. The tea is almost always of a bad, and sometimes of a deleterious quality, the infusion is weak, and little or no milk is added. The operatives return to the mills and workshops until twelve o'clock, when an hour is allowed for dinner. Amongst those who obtain the lowest rates of wages this meal generally consists of boiled potatoes. The mess of potatoes is put into one large dish; melted lard and butter are poured upon them, and a few pieces of fried fat bacon are sometimes mingled with them, and but seldom a little meat. Those who obtain better wages, or larger families whose aggregate income is larger, add a greater proportion of animal food to this meal, at least three times a week; but the quantity consumed by the labouring population is not great. The family sits round the table, and each rapidly appropriates his portion on a plate, or, they all plunge their spoons into the dish, and with an animal eagerness satisfy the cravings of their appetite. At the expiration of the hour, they are all again employed in the workshops or mills, where they continue until seven o'clock or a later hour, when they generally again indulge in the use of tea, often mingled with spirits accompanied by a little bread. Oatmeal or potatoes are however taken by some a second time in the evening.

Some idea of the want of cleanliness prevalent in their habitations, may be obtained from . . . the number of houses requiring white-washing; but this column fails to indicate their gross neglect of order, and absolute filth. Much less can we obtain satisfactory statistical results concerning the want of furniture especially of bedding, and of food, clothing, and fuel. . . . They contain one or two chairs, a mean table, the most scanty culinary apparatus, and one or two beds, loathsome with filth. A whole family is sometimes accommodated in a single bed, and sometimes a heap of filthy straw and a covering of old sacking hide them in one undistinguished heap. . . . Frequently, the inspectors found two or more families crowded into one small house, containing only two apartments, in one of which they slept, and another in which they ate; and often more than one family lived in a damp cellar, containing only one room, in whose pestilential atmosphere from twelve to sixteen persons were crowded. To those fertile sources of disease were sometimes added the keeping of pigs and other animals in the house, with other nuisances of the most revolting character. . . .

The houses of the poor . . . are too generally built back to back, having therefore one outlet, no yard, no privy, and no receptacle for refuse. Consequently the narrow, unpaved streets, in which mud and water stagnate, become the common receptacle of offal and ordure. . . .

These districts are inhabited by a turbulent population, which, rendered reckless by dissipation and want . . . has frequently committed daring assaults on the liberty of the more peaceful portions of the working classes, and the most frightful devestations on the property of their masters. Machines have been broken, and factories gutted and burned at mid-day, and the riotous crowd has dispursed ere the insufficient body of police arrived at the scene of disturbance. . . .

That the various forms of epidemic, endemic, and other disease caused, or aggrevated, or propagated chiefly amongst the labouring classes by atmospheric impurities produced by decomposing animal and vegetable substances, by damp and filth, and close and overcrowded dwellings prevail amongst the population in every part of the kingdom, whether dwelling in separate houses, in rural villages, in small towns, in the larger towns—as they have been found to prevail in the lowest districts of the metropolis.

That such disease, wherever its attacks are frequent, is always found in connection with the physical circumstances above specified, and that where those circumstances are removed by drainage, proper cleansing, better ventilation, and other means of diminishing atmospheric impurity, the frequency and intensity of such disease is abated; and where the removal of the noxious agencies appears to be complete, such disease almost entirely disappears.

That high prosperity in respect to employment and wages, and various and abundant food, have afforded to the labouring classes no exemptions from attacks of epidemic disease, which have been as frequent and as fatal in periods of commercial and manufacturing prosperity as in any others.

That the formation of all habits of cleanliness is obstructed by defective supplies of water.

That the annual loss of life from filth and bad ventilation are greater than the loss from death or wounds in any wars in which the country has been engaged in modern times.

That of the 43,000 cases of widowhood, and 112,000 cases of destitute orphanage relieved from the poor's rates in England and Wales alone, it appears that the greatest proportion of deaths of the heads of families occurred from the above specified and other removable causes; that their ages are under 45 years; that to say, 13 years below the natural probabilities of life as shown by the experience of the whole population of Sweden.

That the public loss from the premature deaths of the heads of families is greater than can be represented by any enumeration of the pecuniary burdens consequent upon their sickness and death.

That, measuring the loss of working ability amongst large classes by the instances of gain, even from incomplete arrangements for the removal of noxious influences from places of work or from abodes, that this loss cannot be less than eight or ten years.

That the ravages of epidemics and other diseases do not diminish but tend to increase the pressure of population.

That in the districts where the morality is the greatest the births are not only sufficient to replace the numbers removed by death, but to add to the population.

That the younger population, bred up under noxious physical agencies, is inferior in physical organization and general health to a population preserved from the presence of such agencies.

That the population so exposed is less susceptible of moral influences, and the efforts of education are more transient than with a healthy population.

That these adverse circumstances tend to produce an adult population short-lived, improvident, reckless, and intemperate, and with habitual avidity for sensual gratifications.

That these habits lead to the abandonment of all the conveniences and decencies of life, and especially lead to the overcrowding of their homes which is destructive to the morality as well as the health of large classes of both sexes.

That defective town cleansing fosters habits of the most abject degradation and tends to the demoralization of large numbers of human beings, who subsist by means of what they find amidst the noxious filth accumulated in neglected streets and bye-places.

That the expenses of local public works are in general unequally and unfairly assessed, oppressively and uneconomically collected, by separate collections, wastefully expended in separate and inefficient operations by unskilled and practically irresponsible officers.

That the existing law for the protection of the public health and the constitutional machinery for reclaiming its execution, such as the Courts Leet, have fallen into desuetude, and are in the state indicated by the prevalence of the evils they were intended to prevent.

12. Master-Serf Relations—Russia

While Britain and other parts of Western Europe were experiencing industrialization, Russia remained overwhelmingly rural. Russia retained serfdom for a generation after most of Europe had abolished this lingering Medieval institution. In this reading, Peter Kropotkin, a famous revolutionary anarchist, recalls the treatment of serfs on his family's estates. The student might wish to compare the status of the Russian serf to the British worker and the black slave in the United States at that time.

Uliana, the housekeeper, stands in the passage leading to father's room, and crosses herself; she dares neither to advance nor to retreat. At last, after having recited a prayer, she enters the room, and reports, in a hardly audible voice that the store of tea is nearly at an end, that there are only twenty pounds of sugar left, and that the other provisions will soon be exhausted.

"Thieves, robbers!" shouts my father. "And you, you are in league with them!" His voice thunders throughout the house. Our stepmother leaves Uliana to face the storm. But father cries, "Frol, call the princess! Where is she?" And when she enters, he receives her with the same reproaches.

"You also are in league with this progeny of Ham; you are standing up for them"; and so on, for half an hour or more.

Then he commences to verify the accounts. At the same time, he thinks about the hay. Frol sent to weigh what is left of that, and our stepmother is sent to be present during the weighing, while father calculates how much of it ought to be in the barn. A considerable quantity of hay appears to be missing, and Uliána cannot account for several pounds of such and such provisions. Father's voice becomes more and more menacing; Uliána is trembling; but it is the coachman who now enters the room, and is stormed at by his master. Father springs at him, strikes him, but he keeps repeating, "Your highness must have made a mistake."

Father repeats his calculations, and this time it appears that there is more hay in the barn than there ought to be. The shouting continues; he now reproaches the coachman with not having given the horses their daily rations in full; but the coachman calls on all the saints to witness that he gave the animals their due, and Frol invokes the Virgin to confirm the coachman's appeal.

But father will not be appeased. He calls in Makár, the piano-tuner and sub-butler, and reminds him of all his recent sins. He was drunk last week, and must have been drunk yesterday, for he broke half a dozen plates. In fact, the breaking of these plates was the real cause of all the disturbance: our stepmother had reported the fact to father in the morning, and that was why Uliána was received with more scolding than was usually the case, why the verification of the hay was undertaken, and why father now continues to shout that "this progeny of Ham" deserves all the punishment on earth.

Of a sudden there is a lull in the storm. My father takes his seat at the table and writes a note. "Take Makár with this note to the police station, and let a hundred lashes with the birch rod be given to him."

Terror and absolute muteness reign in the house.

The clock strikes four, and we all go down to dinner; but no one has any appetite, and the soup remains in the plates untouched. We are ten at table, and behind each of us a violinist or a trombone-player stands, with a clean plate in his left hand; but Mákar is not among them.

"Where is Makár?" our stepmother asks. "Call him in."

Makár does not appear, and the order is repeated. He enters at last, pale, with a distorted face, ashamed, his eyes cast down. Father looks into his plate, while our stepmother, seeing that no one has touched the soup, tries to encourage us.

"Don't you find, children," she says, "that the soup is delicious?"

Tears suffocate me, and immediately after dinner is over I run out, catch Makár in a dark passage, and try to kiss his hand; but he tears it away, and says, either as a reproach or as a question, "Let me alone; you, too, when you are grown up, will you not be just the same?"

D. ECONOMICS

13. Origins of Capitalism, Marx

Karl Marx, if he is second to any man in economics—Adam Smith, is none the less a worthy world economist. And in this selection he is not as abstruse as sometimes. His message is that the middle class capitalist, through the vehicle of usury, money making money, made "with a shove and a kick"—industrial supremacy superbly surpass agricultural-commercial earlier endeavors.

The origin of the industrial capitalist was a less gradual affair than that of the farmer. Doubtless many small guild masters, and yet more independent petty artisans or even wage workers, developed into small capitalists; and later . . . some of them developed into full-blown capitalists. In the infancy of capitalist production, matters often took much the same course as during the early growth of the medieval town system. . . . The snail's pace . . . was by no means accordant with the commercial requirements of the new world market created by the great geographical discoveries at the end of the fifteenth century. But the Middle Ages had handed down two distinct forms of capital. . . . I refer to usurers' capital and merchants' capital.

"At present, all the wealth of society goes first into the possession of the capitalist. . . . He pays the landowner his rent, the labourer his wages, the tax and the tithe gatherer their claims, and keeps a large, indeed the largest . . . share of the annual produce of labour for himself. The capitalist may now be said to be the first owner of all the wealth of the community, though no law has conferred on him the right to this property. . . . This change has been effected by the taking of interest on capital. . . . The power of the capitalist over all the wealth of the country is a complete change in the right of property, and by what law, or series of laws, was it effected?"

In the country districts, the feudal structure of society, and in the towns, the guild organization, hindered the transformation of money capital into industrial capital—the transformation of the money capital that had been formed by means of usury and commerce. These hindrances vanished when feudal society was dissolved. . . . The new manufactures were inaugurated in seaports, or else in parts of the countryside where the old urban system did not run, and where the guilds which were a part of that system had no say. In England, therefore, there was a fierce struggle between the corporate towns and these new industrial nurseries.

14. The Industrial Revolution, Toynbee

The august Toynbee sweepingly described the industrial revolution in theory and in practice.
The theories quickly summed of: Smith, Malthus, Ricardo, Mill, would be enough. But also he deals with the "facts": growth of population, agricultural changes, growth of factories, and not least of all—the thrust of transportation. And it was all revolutionary through the "cash nexus": money gave incredible momentum to what may be the most convincing economic movement of all times: the Industrial Revolution—a pervasive and exciting and inexhaustible thesis.

The essence of the Industrial Revolution is the substitution of competition for the medieval regulations which had previously controlled the production and distribution of wealth. The development of Economic Science in England has four chief landmarks, each connected with the name of one of the four great English economists. The first is the publication of Adam Smith's *Wealth of Nations* in 1776, in which he investigated the causes of wealth and aimed at the substitution of industrial freedom for a system of restriction. The production of wealth, not the welfare of man, was what Adam Smith had primarily before his mind's eye; in his own words, "the great object of the Political Economy of every country is to increase the riches and power of that country." A second stage in the growth of the science is marked by Malthus's *Essay on Population,* published in 1789, which may be considered the product of that revolution, then already in full swing. Adam Smith had concentrated all his attention on a large production; Malthus directed his inquiries, not to the causes of wealth but to the causes of poverty, and found them in his theory of population. A third stage is marked by Ricardo's *Principles of Political Economy and Taxation* which appeared in 1817, and in which Ricardo sought to ascertain the laws of the distribution of wealth. Adam Smith had shown how wealth could be produced under a system of industrial freedom, Ricardo showed how wealth is distributed under such a system. . . . The fourth stage is marked by John Stuart Mill's *Principles of Political Economy,* published in 1848. Mill himself asserted that "the chief merit of his treatise" was the distinction drawn between the laws of production and those of distribution, and the problem he tried to solve was, how wealth *ought* to be distributed. A great advance was made by Mill's attempt to show what was and what was not inevitable under a system of free competition. In it we see the influence which the rival system of Socialism was already beginning to exercise upon the economists. The whole spirit of Mill's book is quite different from that of any economic works which had up to his time been written in England. Though a re-statement of Ricardo's system, it contained the admission that the distribution of wealth is the result of "particular social arrangements," and it recognized that competition alone is not a satisfactory basis of society.

Competition, heralded by Adam Smith, and taken for granted by Ricardo and Mill, is still the dominant idea of our time; though since the publication of the *Origin of Species,* we hear more of it under the name of the "struggle for existence." I wish here to notice the fallacies involved in the current arguments on this subject. In the first place it is assumed that all competition is a competition for existence. This is not true. There is a great difference between a struggle for mere existence and a struggle for a particular kind of existence.

Competition, no doubt, has its uses. Without competition no progress would be possible, for progress comes chiefly from without; it is external pressure which forces men to exert themselves. Socialists, however, maintain that this advantage is gained at the expense of an enormous waste of human life and labour, which might be avoided by regulation. But here we must distinguish, a difference recognized in modern legislation. . . .

Coming to the facts of the Industrial Revolution, the first thing that strikes us is the far greater rapidity which marks the growth of population.

The various factors of primary accumulation may be classed more or less chronologically, and with special reference to certain countries, such as Spain, Portugal, Holland, France and England. In the last named, at the end of the seventeenth century, they were systematically assembled in the colonial system, the national debt system, the modern system of taxation, and the modern system of production. To some extent they rested upon brute force, as, for instance, in the colonial system. One and all, they relied upon the power of the State, upon the concentrated and organized force of society, in order to stimulate the transformation of feudal production into capitalist production, and in order to shorten the period of transition. Force is the midwife of every old society pregnant with a new one. It is itself an economic power.

Under the influence of the colonial system, commerce and navigation ripened like hothouse fruit. Chartered companies were powerful instruments in promotion the concentration of capital. The colonies provided a market for the rising manufactures, and the monopoly of this market intensified accumulation. The treasures obtained outside Europe by direct looting, enslavement, and murder, flowed to the motherland in streams, and were there turned into capital. Holland, the first country to develop the colonial system to the full, had attained the climax of its commercial greatness as early as the year 1648. It was "in almost exclusive possession of the East India trade and the commerce between the south-east and the north-west of Europe. Its fisheries, its mercantile marine, and its manufactures, surpassed those of any other country. The total capital of the republic probably exceeded that of all the rest of Europe put together." Gulich forgets to add that by 1648 the common folk of Holland were more overworked, more impoverished, and more brutally oppressed than those of all the rest of Europe put together.

To-day, industrial supremacy implies commercial supremacy. In the period of manufacture properly so-called, on the other hand, it was commercial supremacy which implied industrial supremacy. Hence the preponderant role of the colonial system in those days. That system was a "strange god" who had mounted the altar cheek by jowl with the old gods of Europe, and who, one fine day, with a shove and a kick, swept them all into the dustbin. The new god proclaimed the making of surplus value to be the sole end and aim of mankind.

Next we notice the relative and positive decline in the agricultural population.

An agrarian revolution plays as large a part in the great industrial change of the end of the eighteenth century as does the revolution in manufacturing industries, to which attention is more usually directed. Our next inquiry must therefore be: What were the agricultural changes which led to this noticeable decrease in the rural population? The three most effective causes were: the destruction of the common-field system of cultivation; the enclosure, on a large scale, of commons and waste lands; and the consolidation of small farms into large. . . . Closely connected with the enclosure system was the substitution of large for small farms. . . . The process went on uninterruptedly into the present century.

Severely, however, as these changes bore upon the rural population, they wrought, without doubt, distinct improvement from an agricultural point of view. They meant the substitution of scientific for unscientific culture.

Passing to manufactures, we find here the all-prominent fact to be the substitution of the factory for the domestic system, the consequence of the mechanical discoveries of the time. Four great inventions altered the character of the cotton manufacture; the spinning-jenny, patented by Hargreaves in 1770; the water-frame, invented by Arkwright the year before; Crompton's mule introduced in 1779, and the self-acting mule, first invented by Kelly in 1792, but not brought into use till Roberts improved it in 1825. None of these by themselves would have revolutionized the industry. But in

1769 . . . James Watt took out his patent for the steam-engine. Sixteen years later it was applied to the cotton manufacture. But the most famous invention of all, and the most fatal to domestic industry, the power-loom, though also patented by Cartwright in 1785, did not come into use for several years, and till the power-loom was introduced the workman was hardly injured.

A further growth of the factory system took place independent of machinery, and owed its origin to the expansion of trade, an expansion which was itself due to the great advance made at this time in the means of communication. The canal system was being rapidly developed throughout the country. In 1777 the Grand Trunk canal, 96 miles in length, connecting the Trent and Mersey, was finished; Hull and Liverpool were connected by one canal while another connected them both with Bristol; and in 1792 the Grand Junction canal, 90 miles in length, made a water-way from London through Oxford to the chief midland towns. Some years afterwards, the roads were greatly improved under Telford and Macadam; between 1818 and 1829 more than a thousand additional miles of turnpike road were constructed; and the next year, 1830, saw the opening of the first railroad. These improved means of communication caused an extraordinary increase in commerce, and to secure a sufficient supply of goods it became the interest of the merchants to collect weavers around them in great numbers, to get looms together in a workshop, and to give out the warp themselves to the workpeople. To these latter this system meant a change from independence to dependence. . . . Another direct consequence of this expansion of trade was the regular recurrence of periods of over-production and of depression, a phenomenon quite unknown under the old system, and due to this new form of production on a large scale for a distant market.

These altered conditions in the production of wealth necessarily involved an equal revolution in its distribution.

The new class of great capitalist employers made enormous fortunes, they took little or no part personally in the work of their factories, their hundreds of workmen were individually unknown to them; and as a consequence, the old relations between masters and men disappeared, and a "cash nexus" was substituted for the human tie. The workmen on their side resorted to combination, and Trades-Union began a fight which looked as if it were between mortal enemies rather than joint producers.

15. Sir Titus Oates—Businessman

The economic message of this businessman who really means business is: "early to rise," utilize punctuality of a military despot, methodical exactness, and withal—economic wholeheartedness. Verve and vitality would seen to be the true marks of business success.

He was a very *early riser,* and his unvarying rule was to be at the works before the engine was started. Is it not written, "the hand of the diligent maketh rich?" and here is a signal illustration of it. It used to be said in Bradford, "Titus Salt makes a thousand pounds before other people are out of bed." Whether the sum thus specified was actually realised by him was cannot say, but it is the habit of early rising we wish to point out, and inculcate on whose business career is about to begin. In these times of artificiality and self-indulgence, when the laws of nature are often dead against those who follow such a course. . . .

It is almost superfluous to mention that this early presence at "the works" exercised a high moral influence over his workpeople. Well they knew they had not merely to do with delegated authority, but with that which was supreme. If any of them were late, it was the master's rebuke they feared. If any were conspicuous above the rest of regularity and skill in their duties, it was the master's approval they expected, and the approval was shown by the promotion of those who served him best. Some who entered his employment in the humblest capacity have been raised to the highest positions in it. There was thus a personal acquaintance formed, and a mutual sympathy established, that greatly helped to bridge the gulf which too often has separated master and workpeople. . . . Throughout his manufacturing career he had great moral power in attaching the workpeople to himself; they all looked up to him as a friend rather than a master. . . .

Another striking feature of his character, and one which enabled him to accomplish so much work, was his punctuality. Never was military despot more rigid than he in the observance of this rule: when he made an engagement he was punctual to the minute and he expected the same in others. . . . Such was his punctuality that he was hardly ever known to miss a train, or to be in a hurry for one. It was the same at home as in business: the hour of meals was observed with precision, and all other domestic arrangements were conducted on the same principle of order. . . .

Another marked characteristic in the prosecution of his immense business was his *methodical exactness:* but for this habit, which was natural to him, he never could have personally controlled the various departments in connection with "the works." He was scrupulously exact in the arrangement of his papers, and knew where to lay his hand on any document when required. His letters were always promptly answered. He was exact in his accounts, exact in the words he spoke—which never had the colour of exaggeration about them—exact in his purchases and sales. When he had fixed his price he stood by it. . . .

But if we were to sum up all the qualities that conducted to his success at this period, all those mental characteristics that enabled him to prosecute his immense business single-handed, it would be expressed in the word *whole-heartedness.*

16. Gospel of Wealth, Carnegie

"The Gospel of Wealth" according to Andrew Carnegie was moral, real, and palpable. The economic price was substantial but the moral and practical rewards boundless. Indeed, Carnegie was the embodiment of morality and money: the only famous saint of rugged economic individualism—the total and replete capitalist!

The problem of our age is the proper administration of wealth, that the ties of brotherhood may still bind together the rich and poor in harmonious relationship. The conditions of human life have not only been changed, but revolutionized, within the past few hundred years. In former days there was little difference between the dwelling, dress, food, and environment of the chief and those of his retainers. . . . The contrast between the palace of the millionaire and the cottage of the laborer with us to-day measures the change which has come with civilization. This change, however, is not to be deplored, but welcomed as highly beneficial. Much better this great irregularity than universal squalor. The "good old times" were not good old times. Neither master nor servant was as well situated then as today.

The price we pay for this salutary change is . . . great. Under the law of competition, the employer of thousands is forced into the strictest economies, among which the rates paid to labor figure prominently, and often there is friction between the employer and the employed, between capital and labor, between rich and poor.

The price which society pays for the law of competition . . . is also great; but the advantages of this law are also greater still than its cost—for it is to this law that we owe our wonderful material development, which brings improved conditions in its train. But, whether the law be benign or not, we must say of it, as we say of the change in the conditions of men to which we have referred: It is here . . . and while the law may be sometimes hard for the individual, it is best for the race, because it insures the survival of the fittest in every department. We accept and welcome, therefore, as conditions to which we must accommodate ourselves, great inequality of environment; the concentration of business, industrial and commercial, in the hands of a few; and the law of competition between these, as being not only beneficial, but essential to the future progress of the race. . . . It is a condition essential to its successful operation that it should be thus far profitable, and even that, in addition to interest on capital, it should make profit. It is a law, as certain as any of the others named, that men possessed of this peculiar talent for affairs, under the free play of economic forces must, of necessity, soon be in receipt of more revenue than can be judiciously expended upon themselves; and this law is as beneficial for the race as the others.

Objections to the foundations upon which society is based are not in order, because the condition of the race is better with these than it has been with any other which has been tried. One who studies this subject will soon be brought face to face with the conclusion that upon the sacredness of property civilization itself depends. . . . Not evil, but good, has come to the race from the accumulation of wealth by those who have had the ability and energy to produce it. But even if we admit for a moment that it might be better for the race to discard its present foundation, Individualism—that it is a nobler idea that man should labor, not for himself alone, but in and for a brotherhood of his fellows, and share with them all in common, . . . even admit all this, and a sufficient answer is, This is not evolution, but revolution. It necessitates the changing of human nature itself—a work of eons, even if it were good to change it, which we cannot know.

. . . Individualism, Private Property, the Law of Accumulation of Wealth, and the Law of Competition . . . these are the highest result of human experience . . . the best and most valuable of all that humanity has yet accomplished. . . .

Poor and restricted are our opportunities in this life, narrow our horizon, our best work most imperfect; but rich men should be thankful for one inestimable boon. They have it in their power during their lives to busy themselves in organizing benefactions from which the masses of their fellows will derive lasting advantage, and thus dignify their own lives.

This, then, is held to be the duty of the man of wealth: To set an example of modest, unostentatious living, shunning display or extravagance; to provide moderately for the legitimate wants of those dependent upon him; and, after doing so, to consider all surplus revenues which come to him simply as trust funds, which he is called upon to administer, and strictly bound as a matter of duty to administer in the manner which, in his judgment, is best calculated to produce the most beneficial result for the community—the man of wealth thus becoming the mere trustee and agent for his poorer brethren, bringing to their service his superior wisdom, experience, and ability to administer, doing for them better than they would or could do for themselves.

In bestowing charity, the main consideration should be to help those who will help themselves; to provide part of the means by which those who desire to improve may do so; to give those who desire to rise the aids by which they may rise; to assist, but rarely or never to do all. Neither the individual nor the race is improved by almsgiving. . . . or in almsgiving more injury is probably done by rewarding vice than by relieving virtue.

Thus is the problem of rich and poor to be solved. The laws of accumulation will be left free, the laws of distribution free. Individualism will continue, but the millionaire will be but a trustee for the poor, intrusted for a season with a great part of the increased wealth of the community, but administering it for the community far better than it could or would have done for itself. The best minds will thus have reached a stage in the development of the race in which it is clearly seen that there is no mode of disposing of surplus wealth creditable to thoughtful and earnest men into whose hands it flows, save by using it year by year for the general good. This day already dawns.

E. SOURCES FOR PART V

1. Alfred Wallace, *Darwinism,* London: 1889.
2. Thomas Huxley, *Evolution and Ethics,* London: the Romanes Lectures, 1893.
3. Frederich Nietzsche, *Beyond Good and Evil,* trans. by Thomas Common, London: 1901.
4. *Translations and Reprints* . . . , I,3.
5. Robinson, *Op.Cit.*
6. Carl Schurz, *Reminiscences,* New York: 1907.
7. *The Annual Register:1849,* London: 1849
8. Karl Marx and Friedrich Engels, *Communist Manifesto,* trans. by Samuel Moore, London: 1881.
9. Otto von Bismarck, *Reflections and Reminiscences,* trans. by A. J. Butler, London: 1898.
10. James P. Kay, *The Moral and Physical Conditions of the Working Classes . . . in Manchester,* London: 1832.
11. *Report from the Poor Law Commissioners on . . . Sanitary Conditions of the Labouring Populations of Great Britain,* London: 1842.
12. Peter Kropotkin, *Memors of A Revolutionist,* 1899.
13. Karl Marx, *Capital,* trans. by Samuel Moore, London: 1886.
14. Arnold Toynbee, *Lectures on the Industrial Revolution,* Rivington: 1884.
15. R. Balgarnie, *Sir Titus Salt, Barone: His Life and Its Lessons,* London: 1877.
16. Andrew Carnegie, *The Gospel of Wealth,* New York: North American Review, 1889.

VI
CONTEMPORARY CIVILIZATION

A. ETHICS

1. Adolph Hitler: Nazi God

The leadership or Führer principle with its emphasis on the unquestioned obedience demanded of the citizen of the Third Reich was an important part of German National Socialist or Nazi ideology. The leader was, of course, Adolph Hitler. This principle is typical of Fascism and other totalitarian ideologies. Selection four is another example.

One of the best expositions of Nazi concept of the Fuhrer principle is given by Huber in his *Constitutional Law of the Greater German Reich:*

"The Führer-Reich of the (German) people is founded on the recognition that the true will of the people cannot be disclosed through parliamentary votes and plebiscites but that the will of the people in its pure and unncorrupted form can only be expressed through the Führer.

"The Führer is the bearer of the people's will; he is independent of all groups, associations, and interests, but he is bound by laws which are inherent in the nature of his people. In this twofold condition: independence of all factional interests but unconditional dependence on the people, is reflected the true nature of the Führer principle. . . . The Führer is no 'representative' of a particular group whose wishes he must carry out. He is no 'organ' of the state in the sense of a mere executive agent. He is rather himself the bearer of the collective will of the people. In his will the will of the people is realized. He transforms the mere feelings of the people into a conscious will. . . . He shapes the collective will of the people within himself and he embodies the political unity and entirety of the people in opposition to individual interests. . . .

"But the Führer, even as the bearer of the people's will, is not arbitrary and free of all responsibility. His will is not the subjective, individual will of a single man, but the collective national will is embodied within him in all its objective, historical greatness. . . .

"In the Führer are manifested also the natural laws inherent in the people: It is he who makes them into a code governing all national activity. In disclosing these natural laws he sets up the great ends which are to be attained and draws up the plans for the utilization of all national powers in the achievement of the common goals. Through his planning and directing he gives the national life its true purpose and value.

"The Führer principle rests upon unlimited authority but not upon mere outward force. It has often been said, but it must constantly be repeated, that the Führer principle has nothing in common with arbitrary bureaucracy and represents no system of brutal force, but that it can only be maintained by mutual loyalty which must find its expression in a free relation.

"That the will of the people is embodied in the Führer does not exclude the possibility that the Führer can summon all members of the people to a plebiscite on a certain question. The purpose of the plebiscite is not to let the people act in the Führer's place or to replace the Führer's decision with the result of the plebiscite. Its purpose is rather to give the whole people an opportunity to demonstrate and proclaim its support of an aim announced by the Führer.

"It would be impossible for a law to be introduced and acted upon in the Reichstag which had not originated with the Führer or, at least, received his approval. The procedure is similar to that of the plebiscite: The law giving power does not rest in the Reichstag; it merely proclaims through its decision its agreement with the will of the Führer, who is the lawgiver of the German people."

"The office of the Führer developed out of the National Socialist movement. It was originally not a state office. . . . The office of the Führer first took root in the structure of the Reich when the Führer took over the powers of the Chancelor, and then when he assumed the position of the Chief of State. But his primary significance is always as leader of the movement; he has absorbed within himself the two highest offices of the political leadership of the Reich and has created thereby the new office of Führer of the people and the Reich."

"The Führer unites in himself all the sovereign authority of the Reich; all public authority in the state as well as in the movement is derived from the authority of the Führer. We must speak not of the state's authority but of the Führer's Authority. . . . The authority of the Führer is complete and all-embracing; it unites in itself all the means of political direction; it extends into all fields of national life; it embraces the entire people, which is bound to the Führer in loyalty and obedience. The authority of the Führer is not limited by checks and controls . . . but it is free and independent, all-inclusive and unlimited. It is derived from the people; that is, it is entrusted to the Führer by the people. It exists for the people and has its justification in the people; it is free of all outward ties because it is in its innermost nature firmly bound up with the fate, the welfare, the mission, and the honor of the people."

2. Communist Ethics, Lenin

Vladimir Ilyich Ulyanov (1870-1924) who used the name Nicolai Lenin as an alias was a leading revolutionary and Marxist theoretician. In 1917 Lenin returned to Russia from Switzerland to play a vital role in the Russian Revolution securing for himself the position of head of the Communist party and dictator of Russia. One aspect of the application of Communist ethics may be seen in selection eight.

You must build up Communist society. In many respects the first half of the work is done. The old is destroyed, as it deserved to be destroyed; it has been transformed into a heap of ruins, as it deserved to be. The ground has been cleared, and on this ground the young Communist generation must build Communist society. You are confronted with the task of construction, and you will be able to cope with it only if you master all modern knowledge, and if you are able to transform Communism from ready-made, memorised formulae, counsels, recipes, prescriptions and programmes into that living thing which unites your immediate work; if you are able to transform Communism into a guide for your practical work.

This is the task by which you should be guided in the work of educating, training and rousing the whole of the your generation. You must be in the first ranks of the millions of builders of Communist society, and every young man and young woman should be such a builder. Unless you enlist the whole mass of young workers and peasants in the work of building Communist society you will not succeed in building it.

Naturally, this brings me to the question of how we should teach Communism and what are the specific features of our methods.

Here, first of all, I will deal with the question of Communist ethics.

You must train yourselves to become Communists. The task of the Young Communist League is to organize its practical activities in such a way that, in learning, organizing, uniting and fighting, it shall train its members and all those who look upon it as their leader, train them to become Communists. The whole object of the training, education and tuition of the youth of today should be to imbue them with Communist ethics.

But is there such a thing as Communist ethics? Is there such a thing as Communist morality? Of course there is. Often it is made to appear that we have no ethics of our own; and very often the bourgeoisie accuse us Communists of repudiating all ethics. This is a method of shuffling concepts, of throwing dust in the eyes of the workers and peasants.

In what sense do we repudiate ethics and morality?

In the sense that they were preached by the bourgeoisie, who declared that ethics were God's commandments. We, of course, say that we do not believe in God, and that we know perfectly well that the clergy, the landlords and the bourgeoisie spoke in the name of God in order to pursue their own exploiter's interests. Or, instead of deducing these ethics from the commandments of morality, from the commandments of God, they deduced them from idealistic or semi-idealistic phrases, which were always very similar to God's commandments.

We repudiate all morality that is taken outside of human, class concepts. We say that this is deception, a fraud, which clogs the brains of the workers and peasants in the interests of the landlords and capitalists.

We say that our morality is entirely subordinated to the interests of the class struggle of the proletariat. Our morality is deduced from the class struggle of the proletariat. . . .

That is why we say that for us there is no such thing as morality taken outside of human society; such a morality is a fraud. For us, morality is subordinated to the interests of the class struggle of the proletariat.

B. LAW

3. Wilson's Fourteen Points—1918

At the end of World War I, Woodrow Wilson presented what he hoped would be a plan for a better tomorrow. Although Germany had agreed to an Armistice based on the Fourteen Points at the peace conference at Versailles the victors were more interested in punishment than justice. The world was still not safe for democracy.

We entered this war because violations of right had occurred which touched us to the quick and made the life of our own people impossible unless they were corrected and the world secure once for all against their recurrence. What we demand in this war, therefore, is nothing peculiar to ourselves. It is that the world be made fit and safe to live in; and particularly that it be made safe for every peace-loving nation which, like our own, wishes to live its own life, determine its own institutions, be assured of justice and fair dealing by the other peoples of the world as against force and selfish aggression. The programme of the world's peace, therefore, is our programme: and as we see it, is this:

I. Open covenants of peace, openly arrived at . . . diplomacy shall proceed always frankly and in the public view.

II. Absolute freedom of navigation upon the seas, outside territorial waters, alike in peace and in war. . . .

III. The removal, so far as possible, of all economic barriers and the establishment of an equality of trade conditions among all the nations consenting to the peace and associating themselves for its maintenance.

IV. Adequate guarantees given and taken that national armaments will be reduced to the lowest point consistent with domestic safety.

V. A free, open-minded, and absolutely impartial adjustment of all colonial claims. . . .

VI. The evacuation of all Russian territory and such a settlenent of all questions affecting Russia as will secure the best and freest cooperation of the other nations of the world in obtaining for her an unhampered and unembarrassed opportunity for the independent determination of her own political development and national policy . . . under institutions of her own choosing. . . .

VII. Belgium, the whole world will agree, must be evacuated and restored, without any attempt to limit the sovereignty which she enjoys in common with all other free nations.

VIII. All French territory should be freed and the invaded portions restored, and the wrong done to France by Prussia in 1871 in the matter of Alsace-Lorraine . . . should be righted. . . .

IX. A readjustment of the frontiers of Italy should be effected along clearly recognizable lines of nationality.

X. The peoples of Austria-Hungary, whose place among the nations we wish to see safeguarded and assured, should be accorded the freest opportunity of autonomous development.

XI. Rumania, Serbia, and Montenegro should be evacuated; occupied territies restored; Serbia accorded free access to the sea. . . .

XII. The Turkish portions of the present Ottoman Empire should be assured a secure sovereignty, but the other nationalities which are now under Turkish rule should be assured an undoubted security of life and an absolutely unmolested opportunity of autonomous development. . . .

XIII. An independent Polish state should be erected which should include the territories inhabited by indisputably Polish populations, which should be assured a free and secure access to the sea. . . .

XIV. A general association of nations must be formed under specific covenants for the purpose of affording mutual guarantees of political independence and territorial integrity to great and small states alike. . . .

. . . An evident principle runs through the whole programme I have outlined. It is the principle of justice to all peoples and nationalities, and their right to live on equal terms of liberty and safety with one another, whether they be strong or weak. Unless this principle be made its foundation, no part of the structure of international justice can stand.

4. The Program of the NSDAP—1920

The era between the two World Wars (1919-39) went from the promised "world safe for democracy" to one of conflicting ideologies. The totalitarian attacks came from both the left and the right. The following is the first program of the German Nazi party.

1. We demand the union of Germans to form a Great Germany on the basis of the right of the self-determination enjoyed by nations.
2. We demand equality of rights for the German People in its dealings with other nations, and abolition of the Peace Treaties of Versailles and St. Germain.
3. We demand land and territory [colonies] for the nourishment of our people and for settling our superfluous population.
4. None but members of the nation may be citizens of the State. None but those of German blood, whatever their creed, may be members of the nation. No Jew, therefore, may be a member of the nation.
7. We demand that the State shall make it its first duty to promote the industry and livelihood of citizens of the State. If it is not possible to nourish the entire population of the State, foreign nationals [non-citizens of the State] must be excluded from the Reich.
8. All non-German immigration must be prevented. We demand that all non-Germans, who entered Germany subsequent to August 2nd, 1914, shall be required forthwith to depart from the Reich.
10. It must be the first duty of each citizen of the State to work with his mind or with his body. The activities of the individual may not clash with the interests of the whole, but must proceed within the frame of the community and be for the general good.

We demand therefore:

11. Abolition of incomes unearned by work.
13. We demand nationalisation of all businesses which have been up to the present formed into companies [Trusts].
14. We demand that the profits from wholesale trade shall be shared out.
15. We demand extensive development of provision for old age.
19. We demand that the Roman Law, which serves the materialistic world order, shall be replaced by a legal system for all Germany.
20. With the aim of opening to every capable and industrious German the possibility of higher education and of thus obtaining advancement, the State must consider a thorough re-construction of our national system of education. The curriculum of all educational establishments must be brought into line with the requirements of practical life. Comprehension of the State idea [State sociology] must be the school objective, beginning with the first dawn of intelligence in the pupil. We demand development of the gifted children of poor parents, whatever

their class or occupation, at the expense of the State.

It must be forbidden to publish papers which do not conduce to the national welfare. We demand legal prosecution of all tendencies in art and literature of a kind likely to disintegrate our life as a nation, and the suppression of institutions which militate against the requirements above-mentioned.

24. We demand liberty for religious denominations in the State, so far as they are not a danger to it and do not militate against the moral feelings of the German race.

25. That all the foregoing may be realized we demand the creation of a strong central power of the State. Unquestioned authority of the politically centralized Parliament over the entire Reich and its organizations; and formation of Chambers for classes and occupations for the purpose of carrying out the general laws promulgated by the Reich in the various States of the confederation.

The leaders of the Party swear to go straight forward—if necessary to sacrifice their lives—in securing fulfillment of the foregoing Points.

5. A Bill of Rights, USSR—1936

There is always the problem between theory and practice. During the period of the Stalin dictatorship, with its secret police, slave labor camps, and other terrorist activities, the Soviet Union had on paper one of the most democratic constitutions.

Fundamental Rights and Duties of Citizens

Article 118

Citizens of the U.S.S.R. have the right to work, that is, the right to guaranteed employment and payment for their work in accordance with its quantity and quality.

The right to work is ensured by the socialist organization of the national economy, the steady growth of the productive forces of Soviet society, the elimination of the possibility of economic crises, and the abolition of unemployment.

Article 119

Citizens of the U.S.S.R. have the right to rest and leisure. The right to rest and leisure is ensured by the establishment of an eight-hour day for industrial, office, and professional workers, the reduction of the working day to seven or six hours for arduous trades and to four hours in shops where conditions of work are particularly arduous; by the institution of annual vacations with full pay for industrial, office, and professional workers, and by the provision of a wide network of sanitoria, holiday homes and clubs for the accommodation of the working people.

Article 120

Citizens of the U.S.S.R. have the right to maintenance in old age and also in case of sickness or disability.

This right is ensured by the extensive development of social insurance of industrial, office and professional workers at state expense, free medical service for the working people, and the provision of a wide network of health resorts for the use of the working people.

Article 121

Citizens of the U.S.S.R. have the right to education.

This right is ensured by universal and compulsory elementary education; by free education up to and including the seventh grade; by a system of state stipends for students of higher educational establishments who excel in their studies; by instruction in schools being conducted in the native language, and by the organization in the factories, state farms, machine and tractor stations, and collective farms of free vocational, technical and agronomic training for the working people.

Article 124

In order to ensure to citizens freedom of conscience, the church in the U.S.S.R. is separated from the state, and the school from the church. Freedom of religious worship and freedom of anti-religious propaganda is recognized for all citizens.

Article 125

In conformity with the interests of the working people, and in order to strengthen the socialist system, the citizens of the U.S.S.R. are guaranteed by law:

a. freedom of speech;
b. freedom of the press;
c. freedom of assembly, including the holding of mass meetings;
d. freedom of street processions and demonstrations.

These civil rights are ensured by placing at the disposal of the working people and their organizations printing presses, stocks of paper, public buildings, the streets, communications facilities and other material requisites for the exercise of these rights.

6. The "Four Freedoms" of Roosevelt—1941

The world was again at war and once more an American president looked upon it as a conflict of democracy against oppression. Roosevelt's four freedoms were an idealistic statement of war aims—more valuable as propaganda than practical.

In the future days, which we seek to make secure, we look forward to a world founded upon four essential human freedoms.

The first is freedom of speech and expression—everywhere in the world.

The second is freedom of every person to worship God in his own way—everywhere in the world.

The third is freedom from want—which, translated into world terms, means economic understandings which will secure to every nation a healthy peacetime life for its inhabitants—everywhere in the world.

The fourth is freedom from fear—which, translated into world terms, means a worldwide reduction of armaments to such a point and in such a thorough fashion that no nation will be in a position to commit an act of physical aggression against any neighbor—anywhere in the world.

This is no vision of a distant millennium. It is a definite basis for a kind of world attainable in our own time and generation. That kind of world is the very antithesis of the so-called new order of tyranny which the dictators seek to create with the crash of a bomb.

To that new order we oppose the greater conception—the moral order. A good society is able to face schemes of world domination and foreign revolutions alike without fear.

Since the beginning of our American history, we have been engaged in change—in a perpetual peaceful revolution—a revolution which goes on steadily, quietly adjusting itself to changing conditions—without the concentration camp or the quick-lime in the ditch. The world order which we seek is the cooperation of free countries, working together in a friendly, civilized society.

This nation has placed its destiny in the hands and heads and hearts of its millions of free men and women; and its faith in freedom under the guidance of God. Freedom means the supremacy of human rights everywhere. Our support goes to those who struggle to gain those rights or keep them. Our strength is our unity of purpose.

To that high concept there can be no end save victory.

7. A Bill of Rights, United Nations—1948

The war was over and new world body was formed. Taking its "Declaration of the Rights of Man" from many of the documents previously presented, the oppressed are once more given hope.

Article 1. All human beings are born free and equal in dignity and rights. They are endowed with reason and conscience and should act towards one another in a spirit of brotherhood.

Article 2. Everyone is entitled to all the rights and freedoms set forth in this Declaration, without distinction of any kind, such as race, colour, sex, language, religion, political or other opinion, national or social origin, property, birth or other status.

Furthermore, no distinction shall be made on the basis of the political, jurisdictional or international status of the country or territory to which a person belongs, whether it be independent, trust, non-self-governing or under any other limitation of sovereignty.

Article 3. Everyone has the right to life, liberty and the security of person.

Article 4. No one shall be held in slavery or servitude; slavery and the slave trade shall be prohibited in all their forms.

Article 5. No one shall be subjected to torture or to cruel, inhuman or degrading treatment or punishment.

Article 6. Everyone has the right to recognition everywhere as a person before the law.

Article 7. All are equal before the law and are entitled without any discrimination to equal protection of the law. All are entitled to equal protection against any discrimination in violation of this Declaration and against any incitement to such discrimination.

Article 8. Everyone has the right to an effective remedy by the competent national tribunals for acts violating the fundamental rights granted him by the constitution or by law.

Article 9. No one shall be subjected to arbitrary arrest, detention or exile.

Article 10. Everyone is entitled in full equality to a fair and public hearing by an independent and impartial tribunal, in the determination of his rights and obligations and of any criminal charge against him.

C. SOCIETY

8. Soviet Justice—1930s

The Bolshevik Revolution of 1917 had successfully defeated its enemies on the battlefield. However, Lenin died in 1924 and was succeeded by Joseph Stalin. Stalin embarked upon a crash program to impose industrialization and his brand of Communism upon Russia. This reading shows the experiences of some of those Russians who ran afoul of Stalin's policies. Were their experiences atypical or typical of Stalinist Russia? Readers might wish to compare Soviet justice to Nazi justice.

A Member of a Russian Collective Farm

I was arrested on January 29, 1933, by the local NKVD authorities without knowing for what. At the interrogation I was accused of agitation against the Soviet power and against the collectivization in the villages. I refused to sign the act of accusation. Then they began to beat me, to threaten me with a pistol, to squash my fingers in the door. But in spite of all I refused to sign. These tortures lasted eight days. After questioning I was sent to Vinnitsa prison, where I remained three months in the Special Corps for political prisoners. The questioning I was subjected to there was more terrible than the first. I was again given the same accusations but refused to sign. I was thrown into a punitive detention cell for 15 days, where conditions were terrible (400 grams of bread and a quart of water a day). Thereafter, for refusing to sign, I was thrown "into the sack"—the most horrible of all tortures in Soviet prison. It consists of the prisoners being tied into a tarpaulin bag, which was pulled tight with straps until the man inside lost consciousness. Blood came out of my mouth and nose. I fainted, then was brought to with cold water. After this torture, I lay in the prison hospital for 15 days but still did not sign the act.

After three months, I was sent to work in the BAM Camp (BaikalAmur Railway) in Siberia. There I was informed of my sentence—six years in concentration camps in distant parts of the U.S.S.R. We worked on clearing the forest; output norms were high. The barracks we lived in were overcrowded by prisoners. It was filthy, the air was bad and plenty of vermin. Mortality was high.

January 31, 1949.   *Name Withheld*

A Red Army Officer

. . . I served my forced labor sentence in a local colony of the NKVD (as existed in all towns), in Kolyma, and in Kikolayevsk-on-the-Amur. At that time there were 500 prisoners in the local colony of the NKVD, 800,000 prisoners in Kolyma and 10,000 prisoners in Nikolayevsk-on-the-Amur.

The working day, including the time required to go to and from work, totaled 12 hours. As a rule, days off were not observed; sometimes only there was no work on afternoons during scheduled days off. Work was done during any weather, and this considerably increased the death rate among the prisoners in the North.

Former Inmates of Soviet Concentration Camps

Food. For those fulfilling their norm, 600 grams of bread, once soup and once groats; for those overfulfilling their norm, 800 grams of bread, and twice soup and once groats; for those underfulfilling their norm, 200 grams of bread, once soup, and grits. Once or twice a week, salted fish; and once or twice a month, meat dishes.

Housing conditions. Long, poorly built barracks, with one or two iron stoves (only around the stoves was it war), with long double-decker cots and a sack filled with straw or sawdust for the prisoner. Congestion, filth, vermin. Once or twice a month, a change of poorly washed clothes.

Winter clothing. Old and worn and dirty cotton mackinaw, cotton trousers, and work shoes. All these conditions create a situation in which the weak are doomed to die and the strong are destined to wither slowly.

In my days, the Kolyma Camp was distinguished for an especially atrocious regime. There all prisoners who could not fulfill their norms for some reason (old age, weakness, lack of training in physical labor) were turned over to special detachments of three so-called *troikas* who, as a rule, sentenced them to be shot, and carried out the sentence, for alleged sabotage, or else lengthened their sentence.

Colonel of the NKVD Garanin was particularly known for his cruelty. He personally and arbitrarily shot prisoners who were not at work for some reason during his visit to a given camp.

The result: yearly 100,000 prisoners were sent to Kolyma, and only about 10,000 returned.

During my stay, the majority of prisoners were workers and peasants. I met among them persons who had been confined for five or six years and still did not know the reason for their arrest and the length of their sentence.

I worked in the camp for about three years, was then released, and directly sent to the front, was surrounded and taken prisoner, and, despite the fact that I never in my life committed any crime against either my country or my people, I cannot return home, as I would be liquidated as an enemy of Stalin.

January 26, 1949   *Alexander Rolin*

9. Herbert Tempest: An Uncommon Common Man

Herbert Tempest, during the summer of 1973, was 81 years of age. He had spent most of his life as an unskilled laborer, a trade-union organizer, and as an activist in the British Labour Party. He was born and lived in a Leeds working-class environment. He had devoted much of his long life trying to improve conditions for the British common people.

In this interview, he related to his granddaughter, her husband, and his wife Milda some of his experiences. The value of this inerview to history is that we have the words, often unlettered and in a thick Yorkshire accent, of a common worker, who related his views on the passage of time and his perception of events. Rather than looking at history from the "top-down," his views give to the student of history a rare glimpse of events from the "bottom looking up." Unfortunately, Herbert Tempest died in February, 1974, but his words leave us with a lasting legacy of an uncommon common man who had passed through an eventful era in Western Civilization.

GD[1]: [Tell us] . . . about your experiences in the Labour Party. Tell me about all of what my mother has told me about you taking her to the Labour meetings. She told me that you took her to a lot of the meetings. Remember? Remember?

H: I remember.

GD: Tell me about that. Because that's history, granddad, and it's important to carry it on. Not to let it go, to carry on.

H: Aye, carry it on.

GS: Please tell us, Herbert.

H: It's just life and what you believe in. There was that much poverty in this country. When I were working in Kitchen's [a locomotive manufacturing concern]. . . . Kitchen's used to turn out about five loco [motives] a week.

1. The following abbreviations are used: GD, granddaughter; GS, grandson; W, Milda, Herbert's wife; H, Herbert Tempest.

There were two thousand on days and there were a thousand on night work—with the world at its feet in locomotive building.

And I seen children, barefooted children, in winter out at 6 o'clock in the morning waiting for scraps of bread that you could bring out to them. And it stunk did this country!

There were more millionaires in this country. . . . We were a rich country, but it were in a few hands.

. . . When the . . . Labour Party started in this country, back in the 1890s, they were thrown in horse ponds and multrated [insulted] with the workers, what they were trying to help. And they were genuine men were those! But as soon as you start getting these high-thinking fellows in—so-called intellectuals—your party is done.

. . . I believed in Labour because I wanted to see poverty wiped away. Why should men be walking around for work and couldn't get none? And they treated you like a dog, you know, in those days when you went to the Labour Exchange [Britain's Government Employment Bureau]. And the more fortunate people among the workers . . . thought that you were lazy—you were nothing. And there was one in ten out of work in this country.

GS: When was this?

W: In the 1930s.

H: And that's the joke I told you. You know bit of a joke about [the man who drowned in a river]. The fellow who went and pulled [the drowned man] . . . out of the river. The fellow said: "I know him! Oh, I'm after his job!" When he got there, the employer said: "I'm sorry, lad. I've just [sit on] hired the man who pushed him in!"

They could take it in that manner, you know. We could stand a joke against ourselves. . . .

Men could be good friends and if on was out of work and a job went available, hoping to get it. The mate said: "Where are you going?" [The other would answer]: "Oh, I'm going to [the bathroom]. But he was going to a firm to get on, but he wouldn't tell him his friend.

GS: Herbert, at that time when you were working for the Labour Party, what did you see? What did you think would happen by your work?

H: I thought a good time were acoming.

GS: For whom?

H: I was disillusioned. I am disillusioned now because of the Labour Party. Every time they've governed this country since the war, they have increased their salaries. This Harold Wilson. He's only an errand boy for the trade unions.

The trade unions has brought this country down to what it is! And who is the trade unions? Working men!

GS: Whose fault is it? Who's wrong? Who's to blame?

H: The workers themselves is to blame.

GS: For what? What didn't they do?

GD: Did they quit too soon? Did they give up just for money? Did they sell out the dream?

H: You know, life is funny. . . . You take it as it comes, what there is.

Now The trade unions, there is a man, been in the newspaper this week. The trade unions, because he wouldn't go out on strike [are trying to expel him]. He said, he told them straight: "You're blacailing the country . . . by force. You're getting colossal wages that you don't earn. And you can't go on like that indefinitely, paying fancy wages!"

There are men earning 40 a week. And then apart from that, if they have four or five kids, they get paid for them [from Britain's family allowance program].

The sound is: "Give me some, give me some, give me some dough!" That's the theme song.

GS: But isn't that what you wanted? Didn't you want more money?

H: Aye, but I didn't want the earth.

GS: You didn't want the earth, but you wanted the sky.

H: Aye.

GS: You wanted the heavens.

H: Aye, but we were always poor. We were poor. Everybody was paid poor wages.

GS: But to the people of that time, didn't you want the heavens? Didn't they think that you wanted the heavens?

H: We all wanted money.

GS: Come on, socialism is not just money.

H: There's nothing in socialism.

GS: . . . That's what you say now. Didn't you think that socialism would make man better? Didn't you want more than just wages?

H: I wanted a bit of money.

GS: Because you thought money would buy you happiness, didn't you?

H: Of course, if we had a job to go to. We didn't bother to save money at times. We'd come home and [listen to the radio]. . . . That was the only things we could do.

GS: Somebody once said, "socialism makes every chef a poet and every poet a chef." Do you believe that?

H: Well, I don't know what you are [politically]. I expect that there are things that you want.

GS: What did you want? That's all.

H: Me, all I wanted was a good meat and potato pie.

GS: But you wanted more. Didn't you want to listen to music after you had eaten the meat and potato pie?

H: Well, I knew there were things I couldn't get.

GS: But you wanted.

H: I'd forget it. I never wanted them. I didn't let it get me down.

I was 57 years old before I ever went for a week's holiday.

GS: You don't begrudge somebody who is 19 and gets all that? Just because you didn't get it until you were 57, you don't care if somebody at 19 gets it. Do you?

W: Oh no!

GD: Granddad, can you tell me how you taught my mom that the "Red Flag"

[Labour Party's official song] flies over Britain?

H: "The people's flag is deepest red/ It shrouded oft our martyred dead/ And ere before their limbs turn stiff and cold. . . ."

What is it now, I forget. But we believed in it. We thought there was something in it.

Now, you've got compulsory communism in Russia. And they're risking their lives to get out of it.

GD: But what you believed in is not communism.

H: It wasn't! It was supposed to be socialism for people to take it and think about it. But communism is false.

GD: Yes, but what you believed in is what the people wanted. Nobody forced it on them.

GS: Herbert, do you believe in capitalism now?

H: I don't know. I believe if a man has got brains and made a fortune [then] he's entitled to it-provided it's not an exploitation.

GS: Now how would you define yourself? You're not a capitalist. You're not a communist. You're not a socialist. What are you now?

H: Well, I know this much: communism is false. They're going to make you think as they want. . . . There's thousands in Siberia at this minute that's there for their beliefs. And . . .

GD: But, granddad, what you believed in. You didn't go to Siberia for. All of Britain has changed for what you believed in. And you can't tell me it's all gone now, because it's still here.

H: Go to the seashore on a fine night and see the sunset. And you'll ask yourself who made it. Somebody did. They've gone to the moon over in America. There's nothing on the moon. You couldn't grow a blade of grass on the moon. . . .

GS: What did you do to bring the people to the moon? What did you do to bring the people to the seashore so that they could see the moon and the sun? So that they could have their holiday once a year too?

H: Nobody knows what life is in the next world, if there is one. So you make the best of this one.

GS: But why didn't you just accept this world? Why did you fight to change it?

H: I fought to change it.

GS: Why? Because you believed in what?

H: Because there was that much poverty.

GS: You wanted it better?

H: I wanted a salary.

GS: Then why can't you accept that it is better? Did you make it better?

H: I'll give you an idea, now. [There was a] a molders and engineers [machinists] strike after the [First World] War. And they'd come out for five shillings a week and they were out six months. And there was no relief and no help, but a soul helping each other.

The miners were out eight months' locked out because they wouldn't accept low wages. And God knows

	wages were low enough. It makes you wonder.
GS:	But if those miners had not gone out, would the miners make the money they do now?
H:	The miners are gone with the aristocrats!
GS:	You know that now, but not at that time.
H:	The miners, the time I'm speaking of, were the finest men in this country. But today they is communists some of them and they are agitators. And they [the miners] let somebody else look after . . . [them].
	Now eventually the communists has got hold of it [the miners' union]. And they are agitators. They can't get a seat on city council. They can't get a seat in House of Commons, but they've done incalculable damage to this country with agitation.
GD:	What about you and Percy Holmes [an old friend and fellow Labourite]?
H:	Percy went right on through [with] it. He died a Labour man. I told him many times, "you're wasting your life."
GS:	What did he believe? Did he think he'd wasted his life?
H:	He got to be secretary in the Labour Party. He thought it was worth it.
GS:	Why did he think it was worth it? And why don't you think it was worth it?
H:	He believed in it, I expect.
GS:	Why did he keep the faith and why didn't you?
H:	Because I saw the corruptness that was creeping into the party.
GS:	Why did Percy keep the faith and not . . . granddad?
W:	Because he [Percy] got a good job. . . . And besides, he was foreman at work and his wife got on the council.
H:	And I recorded [registered] people, who promised to vote Labour and made [through his canvassing] the highest number [of Labour votes] that was ever known in that district.
GS:	You don't vote Labour anymore?
H:	I don't.
GS:	Why did you stop voting Labour?
H:	I got tired one way or the other.
GS:	. . . When you live here, you have to take one side or the other. And he saw all the corruption and how some they got into a job. They get all the family in and they get paid. And another man that's doing the sloughing [hard] work gets nothing.
H:	I went to see Cumberson with a man called Schlisser. He [Cumberson] were after to be an M.P. of the Labour Party [who] had plenty of money—that's been the ruination of the Labour Party. But anyhow, the fellows in . . . [headquarters] were making envelopes and putting a bit of literature in. And they got tired of it, you know from working.
	So this was a friend of Percy Holmes' who was exchequer [treasurer] with a bit of money to give out. I didn't get none. So Percy says: "Why? Is Cumberson taking it all?"

Percy says: "He [Herbert] got 600 votes." [The exchequer] . . . says: "Aye, he doesn't want any. He's enthusiastic!"

The people, even then among the workers, were adventurers who were coming just so to get money. And as soon as they got it, they were off. That's the workers all over. I despise the worker in this country!

W: He worked till he was 76, you know.

GS: Do you vote Conservative now?

H: I vote Conservative due to my old age pension. [The Conservatives do more] than all the talk of the Labour Party.

GS: Do you think you would have gotten the Health Insurance without Labour if they hadn't been around to agitate?

H: I'll tell you what they've done and we have had three Labour governments [since World War II]. They put this country back . . . [by nationalizing] industry. And since 1945, the nationalized industries has fallen into 422 million in debt every year. They're losing now every year. The Post Office lost 64 million last year.

GS: But were nationalized industries supposed to make a profit?

H: They were supposed to, yes.

GS: They were all sick industries except for steel, weren't they?

W: The Post Office was very good.

GS: Post Offices are miserable everywhere, aren't they?

H: It [Post Office] were very good when I were a lad. You could write a letter, say tonight, catch the late post. And let's say it were going to London or to Newcastle, it were delivered the next day for a penny.

GS: When you were a lad, the Post Office was nationalized. Why would it be worse now because Labour was in power in 1945?

H: Wages one thing. . . . There isn't an employee of the Post for ordinary wage earn less than 20 a week. In . . . my day, you had to . . . have two character [references] to be a postman. You had to be in the army or navy. And you had to have two . . . testimonies.

GS: But you couldn't have been a postman then.

H: There's too many gaffers [foreman], too [many] big salaries.

GS: Let me ask you this, Herbert: Wasn't manpower wasted when you were young by maintaining the empire? . . . When you were younger, a lot of people—no goods, noblemen, Conservative voters, middle-class people—went to India, went to the empire and got money for doing nothing too. While you among the working class, didn't get anything.

H: We were exploited.

GS: What's the difference, if now the working class gets some money for doing nothing than when you were young and the middle and upper classes got money for doing nothing?

H: A lot of difference: 'cause I was spending money and they didn't spend at all.

GS: But they were paid for doing nothing. Just as you say [happens] now, people are doing nothing. They were paid from the workers' sweat. And nowadays people are paid from . . . the middle and upper class.

H: How many sweat in this country?

GS: I have no idea. You don't have an empire anymore. That's the problem . . . not so much sweat.

H: There's people here all around about here, I don't care what town it is in this country. You can go into any city or town and there's a dodger [a lazy person] that won't work and he's kept on the fat of the land.

GS: . . . The Labour people keep some dodgers paid and the Conservatives and Liberals used to keep other people paid. Is it any different? It's just you've got different dodgers now.

H: Well, today the so-called big man is getting paid now for to make a speech, put it in the paper, and see what a good man he is. And the people swallow it.

GS: But you used to make speeches for nothing.

H: There were three men in this town when I were a nipper [young] who were millionaires with a million pounds. . . . And the working men were so blinded, they actually turned out because of them being named barons . . . [with] torch light processions. . . . All of them, now, because the man got a million pounds together.
    Well, you can't improve [human nature]. It's a moral standpoint.

GS: Being 81 now, is it better to be 81 now or 81 in the early 1900s?

W: They live better now.

GS: Why?

H: They're getting better food now.

GS: Why are they getting better food? Your daughter had ricketts and hepatitus in the 1930s. . . . Would a child in Britain now have ricketts and hepatitus? And Britain is poorer now than she was then.

H: When she was young all children suffered from hepatitus.

GS: But . . . why don't they now?

H: Now they get plenty of milk.

GS: But why do they have more milk?

H: Because it's produced.

GS: It's not production, it's distribution.

H: All right.

GS: Being an old socialist, [you know] it's distribution, not production. Why is it distributed better now, because of people like you?

H: Well, maybe so. We laid the seed.

GS: . . . If . . . God said to you: "Herbert Tempest, what was your greatest accomplishment for Britain?" What would you answer?

H: Only work, that's all.

GS: But you did more than work. A lot of people worked. A lot of people went along with what happened and accepted, turned their eyes so they couldn't see.

H: I never done a dirty trick, neither a man or woman.

GS: What's dirty?

H: Well. . . .

W: A sneaky trick. Anything sneaky!

GS: You never took advantage of anybody?

H: No.

GS: Have you been taken advantage of?

H: Aye, many times.

GS: By whom?

H: Workers.

GS: Only by workers?

H: Friends.

GS: Only by friends? Only by those people?

GD: Because they wanted your job, granddad? Is it because jobs were so scarce that a man would do his best friend out of a job?

H: Well, you see, you'd be on the job and this was the general way with them the workers: they'd whisper to the gaffer, "Watch, so-and-so." That kind of thing. And fellows are all the same with all trades that curries favors. I never did and I've been sacked because I wouldn't.

GS: You're not saying you've been a fool, are you?

H: Well, I don't know. You can't understand. It's difficult to analyze somebody else's mind. But I always believed in a fair day's work, but at a fair day's wage.

These fellows is what we called clock-watchers, watching clocks go around. And somebody has to make up for them.

GS: Did you believe people were basically good or bad?

H: People were better when I were young than what they are today. . . . Poverty flourished, but we all helped one another. When the children, they couldn't pay an old lady to look after them. . . . Today, it's "how much are you going to give me?" That's the attitude today.

W: Well, everybody, it's time for bed.

D. ECONOMICS

10. The Making of Economic Society, Heilbroner

Robert Heilbroner has the last word on economic patterning, be it: tradition, command, or market. There is no better brief explanation of economics as a whole or capitalism in particular than that of this professional economist and amateur historian. His anticlimactic and unending economic story is a fitting "conclusion" and admonition for economic readings scattered through these readings about Civilization!

The Three Solutions to the Economic Problem

Looking not only over the diversity of contemporary societies, but back over the sweep of all history, he sees that man has succeeded in solving the production and distribution problems in but three ways. That is, within the enormous diversity of the actual social institutions which guide and shape the economic process, the economist divines but three overarching *types* of systems which separately or in combination enable humankind to solve its economic challenge. These great systemic types can be called economies run by Tradition, economies run by Command, and economies run by the Market.

Tradition

. . . by far the most generally prevalent way of solving the economic challenge has been tradition. It has been a mode of social organization in which both production and distribution were based on procedures devised in the distant past, rigidified by a long process of historic trial and error, and maintained by heavy sanctions of law, custom, and belief.

Societies based on tradition solve the economic problems very manageably. First, they deal with the production problem . . . by assigning the jobs of fathers to their sons. Thus a hereditary chain assures that skills will be passed along and that the on-going jobs will be staffed from generation to generation. . . . And it was not merely in antiquity that tradition preserved a productive orderliness within society. In our own Western culture, until the fifteenth or sixteenth centuries, the hereditary allocation of tasks was also the main stabilizing force within society. Although there was some movement from country to town and from occupation to occupation, birth usually determined one's role in life. One was born to the soil or to a trade; and on the soil or within the trade, one followed in the footsteps of one's forebearers.

Thus tradition has been the stabilizing and impelling force behind a great repetitive cycle of society, assuring that society's work would be done each day very much as it had been done in the past. Even today, among the less industrialized nations of the world, tradition continues to play this immense organizing role.

The manner in which tradition can divide a social product may be . . . very subtle and ingenious. It may also be very crude and, by our standards, harsh. Tradition has often allocated to Women, in nonindustrial societies, the most meager of the social product. But however much tradition may accord with or depart from our accustomed moral views, we must see that it is a workable method of dividing society's production.

Traditional solutions to the economic problems of production and distribution are most commonly encountered in primitive agrarian or nonindustrial societies, where in addition to serving an economic function, the unquestioning acceptance of the past provides the necessary perserverance and endurance to confront harsh destinies. Yet even in our own society, tradition continues to play a role in solving the economic problem. It plays its smallest role in determining the distribution of our own social output, although the persistence of such traditional payments as tips to waiters' allowances to minors, or bonuses based on length of service are all vestiges of old traditional ways of distributing goods, as is the differential between men's and women's pay for equal work.

More important is the place which tradition continues to hold, even in America, as a means of solving the production problem—that is, in allocating the performance of tasks. Much of the actual process of selecting an employment in our society is heavily influenced by tradition. We are all familiar with families in which sons follow their fathers into a profession or a business. On a somewhat broader scale, tradition also dissuades us from certain employments. Sons of American middle-class families, for example, do not usually seek factory work, even though factory jobs may pay better than office jobs, because "bluecollar employment" is not in the middle-class tradition.

Even in our society, which is clearly not a "traditional" one, custom provides an important mechanism for solving the economic problem. But now we must note one very important consequence of the mechanism of tradition. *Its solution to production and distribution is a static one.* A society which follows the path of tradition in its regulation of economic affairs does so at the expense of large-scale rapid social and economic change.

Command

A second manner of solving the problem of economic continuity also displays an ancient lineage. This is the method of imposed authority, of economic command. It is a solution based not so much on the perpetuation of a viable system by the changeless reproduction of its ways, as on the organization of a system according to the orders of an economic commander-in-chief.

Not infrequently we find this authoritarian method of economic control superimposed upon a traditional social base. Thus the Pharaohs of Egypt exerted their economic dictates above the timeless cycle of traditional agricultural practice on which the Egyptian economy was based. By their orders, the supreme rulers of Egypt brought into being the enormous economic effort which built the pyramids, the temples, the roads.

The mode of authoritarian economic organization was by no means confined to ancient Egypt. We encounter it in the despotisms of medieval and classical China which produced,. among other things, the colossal Great Wall or in the slave labor by which many of the great public works of ancient Rome were built. Of course, we find it today in the dictates of the communist economic authorities. In less drastic form, we find it also in our own society, for example, in the form of *taxes*—that is, in the preemption of part of our income by the public authorities for public purposes.

Economic command, like tradition, offers solutions to the twin problems of production and distribution. In times of crises, such as war or famine, it may be the only way in which a society can organize its manpower or distribute its goods effectively. Even in America, we commonly declare martial law when an area has been devastated by a great natural disaster. On such occasions we may press people into service, requisition homes, impose curbs on the use of private property such as cars, or even limit the amount of food a family may consume.

To be sure, economic command which is exercised within the framework of a democratic political process is very different from that which is exercised by strong-arm methods: there is an immense social distance between a tax system controlled by Congress and outright expropriation or labor impressment by a supreme and unchallengeable ruler. Yet whilst the means may be much milder, the *mechanism* is the same. In both cases, command diverts economic effort toward goals chosen by a higher authority. In both cases it interferes with the existing order of production and distribution, to create a new order ordained from "above."

The Market

There is also a third solution to the economic problem—that is, a third solution to the problem of maintaining socially viable patterns of production and distribution. This is the *market organization of society,* an organization which, in truly remarkable fashion, allows society to insure its own provisioning with a minimum of recourse either to tradition or command.

Because we live in a market-run society, we are apt to take for granted the puzzling—indeed, almost paradoxical-nature of the market solution to the economic problem. But assume for a moment that we could act as economic advisors to a society which had not yet decided on its mode of economic organization. Suppose, for instance, that we were called on to act as consultants to one of the new nations emerging. . . .

We could imagine the leaders of such a nation saying, "We have always experienced a highly tradition-bound way of life. Our men hunt and cultivate the fields and perform their tasks as they are brought up to do by the force of example and the instruction of their elders. We know, too, something of what can be done by economic command. We are prepared, if necessary, to sign an edict making it compulsory for many of our men to work on community projects for our national development. Tell us, is there any other way we can organize our society so that it will function successfully—or better yet, more successfully?"

Suppose we answered, "Yes, there is another way. Organize your society along the lines of a market economy."

"Very well," says the leaders. "What do we then tell people to do? Now do we assign them to their various tasks?"

"That's the very point," we would answer. "In a market economy no one is assigned to any task. The very idea of a market society is that each person is allowed to decide for himself what to do."

"In a market society, all the jobs will be filled because it will be to people's advantage to fill them."

Our respondents accept this with uncertain expressions. "Now look," one of them finally says, "let us suppose that we take your advice and let our people do as they please. Now let's talk about something important, like cloth production. Just how do we fix the right level of cloth output in this 'market society' of yours?"

"But you don't," we reply.

"We don't! Then how do we know there will be enough cloth produced?"

"There will be," we tell him. "The market will see to that."

"Then how do we know there won't be *too much* cloth produced?" he asked triumphantly.

"Ah, but the market will see to that too!"

"But what *is* this market that will do all these wonderful things? Who runs it?"

"Oh, nobody runs the market," we answer. "It runs itself. In fact there really isn't any such *thing* as 'the market.' It's just a word we use to describe the way people behave."

"But I thought people behaved the way they wanted to!"

"And so they do," we say. "But never fear. They will want to behave the way you want them to behave."

"I am afraid," says the chief of the delegation, "that we are wasting our time. We thought you had in mind a serious proposal. But what you suggest is madness. It is inconceivable. Good day, sir."

E. SOURCES FOR PART VI

1. U.S. Department of State, *National Socialism,* Washington: Govt. Printing Office, 1943.
2. U.S. House of Representatives. Committee on Foreign Affairs, *The Strategy and Tac-*

tics of Communism, Washington: Govt. Printing Office, 1948.
3. U.S. Congress, *Congressional Record,* Washington: Govt. Printing Office, 1920.
4. U.S. Department of State, *National Socialism.*
5. Sir Bernard Pares, "Text of the New Constitution of the U.S.S.R.," *International Conciliation* (Feb., 1937), Carnegie Endownment for International Peace.
6. U.S. Congress, *Congressional Record,* 1941.
7. United Nations, "Universal Declaration of Human Rights." (General Assembly Resolution 217 A (III) of 10 December, 1948).
8. *Slave Labor in Russia: The Case Presented by the American Federation of Labor to the United States,* n.p., 1949.
9. Interview by Donald Haley. 1973.
10. Robert L. Heilbroner, *The Making of Economic Society*, 2nd ed. ° 1968. Reprinted by permission of Prentice Hall, Inc.; Englewood Cliffs, N. J.